# The Connoisseur
# UP NORTH

## A Food-Lover's Guide to Northern Michigan

Sherri and Graydon DeCamp

**bay**Shore Partners  /  **bay**Shore Books
Elk Rapids, Michigan          Publishers

**Art Director**: Thomas Kachadurian
**Illustration**: Tim Ellyson
**Cover photograph concept**: Sherri DeCamp
**Cover photograph**: Copyright © 1995 by Thomas Kachadurian

Inquiries and orders:
Bayshore Books
P. O. Box 549, Elk Rapids, MI 49629
Fax: 616/264-6193, or E-mail to: baypartner@aol.com

PRINTED IN THE UNITED STATES of AMERICA

To our parents, Jimmy and Anne,
Paul and Marjorie, who taught
us that mealtimes are not just
for sustenance, but are
occasions for celebrating
conversation and kinship.

# Table of Contents

# Chefs' Cookbook

# Foreword

My, but we've come a long way! When I first opened the Rowe in 1972, the North could best be described as a culinary wasteland, with broiled whitefish and prime rib passing for fine cooking. Now, 23 years years later, the restaurants and cuisine in this land Up North are good enough, numerous enough, and important enough to warrant a fine book. It has been a marvelous evolution, and I am proud of the Rowe's small part in making it happen.

The success of all of Northern Michigan's fine restaurants would never have occurred, however, without the thousands of knowledgeable people who appreciated good food and wine and who supported all of us by patronizing our restaurants.

Two of the most passionate among them are Graydon and Sherri DeCamp. These two love great food and wine, and have a keen eye for both. The Rowe has been written up hundreds of times over the years, but no one has ever captured the essence of what we do better than Graydon and Sherri. Believe me, you can trust what they tell you about dining Up North. If you love food and wine—and Northern Michigan—as much as I do, you need this book.

—*Wes Westhoven*
*The Rowe*

# Foreword

The main reason I choose to be involved with food and wine as "life" is that this is a constantly changing profession. There are always new food combinations to experience, new preparations, new vintages. Some of the most memorable and enjoyable times in life come while we are sharing good foods and wines.

It is entirely appropriate that writers share these passions, and I welcome being included in a book by Sherri and Graydon DeCamp. As residents of the area they are familiar with the vagaries of the inherently seasonal restaurant business in Northwest Michigan. They cook, they dine out, and they are passionate about great food and wine.

To me, the best restaurant "review" is a literate description of what a restaurant sets out to achieve. Rather than awarding an arbitrary number of stars or toques, it gives readers the details necessary to make judgments on their own. It follows that instead of writing negatively of a particular establishment, the best policy is simply not to write about it at all. It means a great deal to be included in a discriminating book whose authors make enlightened, articulate observations about fine dining.

—*Harlan "Pete" Peterson*
*Tapawingo*

# Introduction

Among the pleasures of writing a monthly restaurant column for a magazine like *Traverse* is the adventure of seeking new experiences. Adventure, of course, is something people come to Northern Michigan for, be it sailing to the Manitous, hiking a new stretch of trail, or finding a new artist whose work you like. We enjoy doing all these things, which is why this a such wonderful place to live. And as food-lovers, we find every bit as much adventure in seeking out new and interesting restaurants and recipes.

Northern Michigan is just the place for the food-loving adventurer. This may come as something of a surprise if you haven't spent much time Up North lately. Historically speaking, the area is better known for landscape than linguine, and its attractions are more obvious to the skier or angler than to the epicure. Not too many years ago this was a land of loggers and homesteaders, and even after it became popular for its resorts, "gourmet" dining often meant little more than a clean tablecloth and planked whitefish.

That's hardly the case any more. Thousands of long-time summer visitors have now become year-round residents, and each week brings more young professionals north from the big cities in search of a gentler place to live, work, and bring up children. Many of them come equipped with discriminating tastes and decidedly cosmopolitan expectations. This is one reason why the still-rustic northern landscape now supports the trappings of urban culture out of all proportion to its population. Northern Michigan today is awash in poets, writers, artists, and craftsmen. It has a long tradition of fine music anchored by the world-famous Interlochen Arts Academy, and now boasts a professional symphony and lively, year-round jazz and chamber-music organizations. Along with such fine things, of course, goes an appreciation for good food. Being resort country, Northern Michigan has a strong hospitality-industry tradition which offers inventive, imaginative new chefs a solid foundation to build on. The result is that there is real culinary adventure these days Up North.

Some of the area's restaurants are known far beyond the North Woods. A few years ago the minuscule town of Ellsworth and its two world-class rest-aurants, The Rowe and Tapawingo, were featured in *Time* magazine. This year a national survey named them the two best restaurants in all of Michigan, and cited four other Northern Michigan establish-ments among the state's top ten. All this attention is well-deserved of course, but singling out a few slights many other fine, if less visible, restaurants that go quietly about their business, serving up exquisite, inventive meals in glorious surroundings for an appreciative local clientele. Seeking them out is wonderful fun.

No two Northern Michigan restaurants are alike. They range from waterfront bistros to skyscraper rooftops, from elegant white-tablecloth establishments to country roadhouses as knotty-pine casual as they were back in the days when you could catch your limit of two-pounders before lunch. Given the variety, people often ask us for guidance on where to take house-guests or what the best place is for some particular dish. This book is an attempt to address such questions.

Note that we say "address" rather than "answer." To ask which restaurant is "best" is like asking which poem is best, or which painting or which sunset. Tastes vary too much for any one person to judge. Besides, the last thing we want to do is tell you where to go. Our tastes aren't yours, and we encourage you to use this book only as a guide and to go adventuring yourself to find your own answers.

Our first and foremost yardstick in gauging restaurants is quite subjective: All the establishments we mention in this book are places we would take friends when they come to visit. We know the proprietors and chefs. We have enjoyed their food and tasted from their cellars, and we have visited them in their kitchens and talked shop. These are all good restaurants, although not always for the same reasons, and we don't hesitate to send you there.

Subjectivity aside, we do apply some standards. If we didn't, you'd learn nothing here that you couldn't learn

reading the phone book. You won't find any chain outlets or franchises in our book, nor any places that rely heavily on stuff that comes off a truck frozen, canned or prepackaged. All restaurants, of course, deal to some degree with the food-service jobber, but the good chefs use fresh, natural, ingredients whenever they can and prefer indigenous products even if they do live in a place that's knee-deep in snow much of the year.

We present our culinary adventures geographically, with sections on four general areas (Leelanau-Benzie; Grand Traverse; Charlevoix-Elk-Torch-Boyne; Petoskey-Harbor Springs). We begin each section by profiling restaurants there which we consider first-rate in all respects. Then we offer somewhat briefer comments about a few of our favorites for "other seasons, other reasons." The latter are either closed much of the year or commendable for one particular attribute or other.

The restaurants we have chosen to profile at length have certain things in common. All meet the subjective test we discussed above, of course, and all are assiduous and inventive when it comes to the selection, preparation, and presentation of food. With few exceptions, you will find the owner present on a daily basis, either at the door or in the kitchen, for it is as difficult to run a good restaurant *in absentia* as it is to paint a fine landscape from a snapshot. The very best restaurants tend, too, to have staffs that are gracious but unpretentious, knowledgeable but unobtrusive, who neither rush nor delay you, and who never let the inevitable detritus of a long meal accumulate on the tables. (We concede that we will always have servers bent on first-name acquaintanceships, especially in summer when students flood the market. Face it, this is not the big city, and such friendly informality is downright charming if not overdone. In the best restaurants Up North, however, your server will exhibit restraint, even if she is your stockbroker's daughter.)

We believe, too, that good food deserves good wine. Wine enhances food, enlivens conversation and, in reasonable amounts, promotes health. For this reason, all of our fully featured restaurants have wine lists worthy of the name, and some have entire walls of framed *Wine Spectator* awards. (If you don't know it already, you will also discover in this book that some of the wines poured in these restaurants are truly *vins du pays*, for the same blessings of soil and climate that make Northern Michigan the world's cherry capital now support vineyards and wineries that produce some pleasant whites.)

For us to regard a restaurant as first-rate in "all respects" it must also be a year-round establishment. We have nothing against places that hang out signs each October saying "See you in the spring!" Many of them are fine restaurants when they are open, and we know that there simply isn't enough business in the off-season for them all to remain open, especially in remote places. Still, we who

live in Northern Michigan year-round appreciate businesses that are here year-round, too. Granted, they may adjust their hours from season to season, or even close for a few weeks at certain times of year. Closing in April to gird for another summer is as much a way of life Up North as closing in November to go hunting. (For all these reasons, whenever you dine out Up North, it is always best to call ahead—in summer, to make reservations, and the rest of the year just to be sure they're open.) Our admitted bias in favor of year-round businesses means that no matter how wonderful the food or service, seasonal restaurants appear among our choices for "other seasons, other reasons." These establishments vary from Mackinac's majestic Grand Hotel with its well-drilled battalions of uniformed Jamaican waiters, to the cool, laid-back intimacy of little Northern Delights Cafe in Benzonia. Both are first-rate, but both are closed much of the year.

So much for "other seasons." What do we mean by "other reasons?" What we mean is that good food is hardly limited to trendy, pricey establishments, or even to full-service restaurants with table service and long wine lists. Some very fine, interesting, inventive dishes await you in cafes, bistros, taverns, roadhouses and coffeehouses that have never seen a white tablecloth. They're simpler places, perhaps, but consider the virtues of simplicity. Price, of course, is one. Another is informality. Granted, we don't have many snooty maitre d's to contend with anywhere in Northern Michigan, but some of the "finer" restaurants might make you uncomfortable in jeans (especially the one holdout that still requires gentlemen to wear a coat and tie). We think food-lovers want to know about places where they can be at ease with their hair in crushed disarray after a day's skiing. At places we suggest for "other reasons," the accepted dress likely runs to Levi's and buffalo plaid. You'll probably not find two escargots to rub together, and the wine list (if there is one) may be short. But at such places we have found world-class fare, from quiches and pub-lunch salads to ribs, whitefish, perch, burgers, soup and pie.

Just keep in mind, please, that some of the restaurants of which we write are included as much for what and where they are as for what they serve. We are confident that as long as you don't expect them to be something they are not, not one will disappoint you.

Even if you've lived in Northern Michigan for years, we hope you'll find restaurants in this book you've not been to before, and maybe even a few you've never heard of. We urge you to get off your own beaten paths and try some places that are new to you. This is what adventure is all about. And if your favorite restaurant is not in this book, please don't assume we think ill of it. We don't pretend to have been to every place in Northern Michigan. This book is simply our way of telling you about the ones we know well and like best.

Finally, remember that we all have our personal preferences. Our taste, frankly, runs to light fare and modest servings. We don't enjoy food that is deep-fried, greasy, or served in heroic amounts. To us, less is more, and we'd rather finish a meal a bit hungry than too stuffed to walk comfortably. Perhaps you, on the other hand, prefer heaps of sticky-sweet ribs and don't give a hoot about wine or care whether your salad is arugula or iceberg. That's fine with us, and we assure you there's something in this book for you, too.

What we hope above all, as you go adventuring in Northern Michigan, is that we'll help you find, right around the next bend, one of those special little restaurants with outstanding food, a good glass of wine, a friendly proprietor, and that unmistakable Up North atmosphere of pine paneling, a stone fireplace, a screen porch, and a sunset over water.

*Sherri & Graydon DeCamp*
*Elk Rapids, Michigan*

# Leelanau-Benzie

The Benzie-Leelanau region, perhaps the Lower Peninsula's most scenic, is famous for dramatic dunes soaring 400 feet above Lake Michigan. Among them are charming coastal fishing and resort villages, and inland, the hills are covered with meadows, forests and well-combed orchards.

The scenic focus is Sleeping Bear Dunes National Lakeshore, 22 miles of coast worth at least a day of any visitor's time. Its hiking and skiing trails will let you work up a powerful appetite. But first, stop and see the informative Visitor's Center in Empire, where you'll also find a local historical museum with a one-room schoolhouse and a 1900 saloon. A few miles north, off M-109, are the spectacular overlooks of Pierce Stocking Drive and a 300-foot sand pile called the "Dunes Climb" at the start of a 1.5-mile trail over the dunes to the beach. Nearby at tiny Glen Haven are a maritime museum with a restored 19th-century life-saving station, and a shoreline where you can still find bits and pieces of century-old shipwrecks.

Good cycling is everywhere, with lakes of all shapes and sizes to ride around. Glen Lake is especially scenic and ringed by roads with wide, paved shoulders. Benzie's Crystal Lake affords a mostly level, 22-mile circuit and a beautiful spur to Point Betsie and its dramatic lighthouse. Canoeists can paddle the Platte, and in winter there are downhill skiing at Crystal Mountain, the Homestead and Sugar Loaf, and cross-country trails in the National Lakeshore and at Leelanau State Park near Northport.

Accommodations in Leelanau tend to be informal and not grand in scale, with numerous inns and quiet B&Bs, and two charming restaurants with guest rooms.

In Leland is quaint old Fishtown, once home port to a commercial fishing fleet. Now the shanties and smokehouses are gift shops and galleries, and a restaurant and inn overlook the docks. Also in Leland is a "Cultural Center" in what was once an art school, where colorful paint splatters left on the floor by generations of art students have been as lovingly preserved as the white frame building itself. The library and historical museum next door always have something fun to offer for rainy days.

And if you still have time before dinner, there's a beautifully restored lighthouse at the tip of the peninsula from which you can see all the way to Charlevoix, three counties away. Oh, go ahead. Remember, it stays light pretty late Up North in summer, so there's lots of time to do it all before you sit down to that wonderful meal you've been looking forward to.

# La Bécasse

Peachy and John Rentenbach's little 40-seat restaurant near Glen Arbor is the perfect combination for food adventurers, if only because of the adventures the proprietors have had in providing us with their superb French country cooking.

They first time they saw the place was as guests in 1987, while visiting the area in connection with Peachy's job at the time as executive director of the Michigan Restaurant Association. When she got back home downstate, she wrote the owner, Mary Ann O'Neil, to ask how the restaurant was going. She was somewhat surprised to get a letter back asking, "How did you know it was for sale?" Next thing Peachy and John knew they had chucked their jobs and bought La Bécasse.

"We had some start," she remembers. "We moved up North in the middle of a blizzard. On our very first night at the restaurant I curdled the *crème brûlée* and the roof in the men's room sprang a leak." She handled it with aplomb, just as she's been handling La Bécasse ever since. "I took the *crème brûlée* off the menu, and just asked everyone to use the ladies'."

On their first New Year's Eve, she remembers, "The chef was carving pheasant breast, and he skewered his hand. He tried to keep working because we had a full house of reservations, but John insisted on taking him to the hospital. So there I was, the only person left in the place, with nothing ready and 120 people coming for dinner. I bravely walked into the kitchen, and all I could find was a list that said 'leek, potato, shrimp.' Luckily, they got back in time to save me."

What you'll find at La Bécasse today is a perfectly prepared meal from a fine kitchen that's placid by comparison. The headiest adventures at La Bécasse nowadays spring from the skills that chef Greg Murphy applies to Peachy's classic notions of French country cooking. The fare is rich with Gallic consommés, remoulade and ratatouille, timbales, pâtés and galantines. Here you'll find grilled *escalopes de veau*, tournedoes of beef in red wine, chicken breasts with basil mousse in *croustades* of potato. She allows an occasional exception to French rule. After all, not even a fanatic Gaullist could succeed in Northern Michigan without the ubiquitous whitefish. La Bécasse, however, adds French

accents that the old-time gill-netters would never have recognized, such as baking the whitefish with bread crumbs, black olives, herbs and lemon *beurre blanc.*

La Bécasse's menu, which changes weekly, frequently includes game, and the Rentenbachs delight in accommodating special orders. "It's fun to make what customers request," she says. "We have one who always calls ahead and asks for elk."

*Bécasse* means "woodcock," but journalistic integrity requires us to report that *bécasse* is also an old French slang term for a naive, gullible woman. What that has to do with anything is beyond us, however, because even if this is their first restaurant, Peachy is no neophyte. Before her restaurant-association days, she was a food columnist for the *Free Press* and a recipe tester for Kraft. She makes the desserts customers enjoy so much—the profiteroles, the white chocolate mousse and raspberry sauce, and the hazelnut pudding and *crème Anglaise.*

The appearance of La Bécasse is simple, austere, and appropriately crisp with the frugality of French peasant life. A simple drapery separates foyer from

---

## La Bécasse

9001 S. Dunns Farm Rd.
Burdickville
616/334-3944

Appetizers about $6
Salads $3-4
Entrees generally $17-25
Wines $16-60

---

dining area, and the walls of whitewashed masonry are adorned by a few unimposing paintings. At La Bécasse, as in, say, the storied foothills of *le Massif Central*, it is what comes from the kitchen that matters.

The cellar, as you'd expect, is heavily French, and favors the regions that gave us classic "French" cooking, Beaujolais and Burgundy. There are clarets for balance, however, and a few Californias and local wines as well. Most important, we have found that Mme. R. not only enjoys talking about her food, but is quite reliable when it comes to suggesting wines to go with it.

---

## Recipes

# The Bluebird

L eland is one of those tradition-steeped resort towns to which loyal cottagers have been returning for generations, and a few elders among them still remember watching outdoor movies on Saturday nights at the Bluebird Tea Room, as Martin and Leone Telgard named it when they opened in 1927.

Prohibition's gone now, and the 'Bird is no longer a tea room, but it is certainly one of the traditions folks return to Leland for. It is run today by Martin and Leone's grandsons: Cris is the chef, and Skip tends to the front of the house. The Bluebird evolved in stages, from tea room to coffee and sandwich shop, to burger joint, to bar, to restaurant.

The 'Bird has a sort of dual personality: The spacious dining room in back seats 180 and has picture windows overlooking the grassy, willow-lined banks of the Leland River. The bar up front is all pine-paneled casual, with cozy window booths, the steady hum of happy conversation among the Leelanau regulars, and the game du jour on TV over the bar.

Ever since tourists discovered Leland and its ineffably quaint Fishtown in the 1960s, the 'Bird has been more than just

busy much of the year. In summer, don't even think about dinner in the restaurant without a reservation. In the bar it's okay just to show up and hope, and if you find yourself in for a bit of a wait, it's no matter, because you'll quickly be deep in conversation with others who are waiting with you. Off-season, the 'Bird can sometimes seem just as crowded because only the bar is open during the week.

Frankly, we think the best bet at the 'Bird is the bar, whose menu leans to burgers and fries, soup and sandwiches, ribs and salad. After a day of biking or skiing in the lovely Leelanau countryside, we consider it a special treat to chow down there on a platter of whitefish, fries and slaw, which is about as fancy as the fare gets.

The main restaurant is another story altogether, with a full and quite sophisticated menu. We particularly remember a snowy weekend that included a fine dinner there of mussels steamed in wine and herbs, scallops sautéed with olives, tomatoes and onions, and served over penne with feta and parsley.

The Telgards reward year-round regulars with

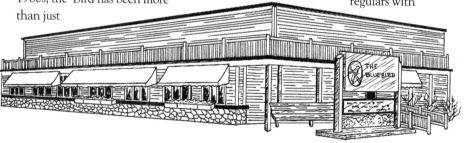

delightful off-season specials, most notably their "ethnic feast" nights in the bar on Wednesdays and Thursdays. The ethnicity changes week to week, but it is always a bargain at a price that hovers around $15. Prices are even gentler on Tuesday "budget nights" when you might find lasagna for $6.95, or a burger with fries for $2.50. The 'Bird also puts on an annual benefit brunch for the Leland Art Center and a "Blues Night" benefit for every local's favorite cause, the Leelanau Conservancy.

Like so many Northern Michigan restaurants, the Bluebird claims to be famous for whitefish, and here it is a solid claim whose pedigree goes back to Leone's day. The filets are still individually chosen, trimmed and pin-boned, and for $12.95 you can have it any of three ways: broiled with lemon-butter, blackened, or "Bluebird style." The latter is the classic, dusted with seasoned flour and fried in

---

## The Bluebird
## Restaurant and Bar

102 E. River St., Leland
616/256-9081

Dinners generally $11-16
(incl. soup or salad)
Appetizers $4-5 extra
Wines $12-28
Bar dinners $7-10

---

clear, light oil.

Also on the agenda in the restaurant are the magnificent cinnamon rolls Leone started making about 60 years ago. Until recently they were rationed, one to a customer, because the Bluebird's oven was so small. Now they have a new oven big enough to make you seconds and have enough left over to sell you a sack to take home.

# Recipes

# Hattie's

Behind its simple, unobtrusive facade in Suttons Bay's business district, Hattie's subdued decor and quiet elegance provide a perfect setting for some of Northern Michigan's most inventive and interesting cuisine.

When Jim Milliman opened Hattie's in 1987, after having been chef at The Rowe in Ellsworth, he shifted gears from the regional, French style and adopted the global influences streaming east from California, with their inscrutable combinations of flavors and exquisitely artistic presentation. Milliman is an agent of change, and Hattie's offers cutting-edge cuisine.

Almost everything about Hattie's is understatement—soft lighting, restful grey tones. It helps concentrate the senses, and provides a nice foil for the art on the walls, which changes monthly because Hattie's doubles as a gallery for Michigan artists' work.

The regular clientele tends to care very much about food, so Milliman enjoys revealing a bit about ingredient and method on his menus. It makes for fun reading if difficult choices. "Grilled Rack of Venison," read one recent menu entry, "marinated in olive oil, then char-grilled. It is served with a tart cherry BBQ sauce and presented with garlic mashed potatoes." Even so, not all is revealed; behind the words "BBQ sauce" lie onions and garlic carefully sautéed in sesame oil and simmered 30 minutes with vinegar, tomato ketchup, fresh cherries and cherry preserves, brown sugar, light molasses, ginger, red pepper, Worcestershire, and cumin seed.

Milliman understands, too, that Northern Michigan diners treasure their favorite foods, so he usually offers a whitefish dish as well as some exquisitely prepared pork or beef. He also always has fat-free and vegetarian dinners, and puts no less thought and artistry into them than into the most complexly prepared, grilled lamb. A recurring no-fat favorite is Pacific salmon, poached with vegetables in a *court-bouillon* and seasoned with basil and oregano. Even the most determined carnivore could be lured by his vegetarian delights, such as roasted red-pepper and cheese souffle, served with a fennel broth and sprinkled with grated cheese.

Our first meal at Hattie's, some years ago soon after it opened, was on one of those typical Up North occasions when the restaurant at which we had intended

to eat turned out to be closed. So we tried "that new place," Hattie's, instead. We were somewhat surprised to find ourselves in a rather urban atmosphere, devoid of knotty pine, stone hearth, or view of the bay, but rich in quiet elegance, muted conversation and delicious aroma. Hattie's, we discovered to our delight, is about food.

And wine, of course. The comprehensive cellar is nicely balanced between red and white, New World and Old; the major French regions are represented, as is Northern Michigan, and a nice variety is offered by glass as well as bottle. An annual tradition at Hattie's is the Beaujolais Nouveau tasting in November.

Milliman also offers periodic "cookbook" dinners through the off-season, and locals enjoy pre-theater, *prix fixe* dinners before the flicks at the Bay across the street. For light diners, some entrees are occasionally offered half-portion at sharp discount. We veteran grazers enjoy the nights when a salad and any two appetizers can be ours for $18, because Milliman's appetizers are as remarkable as his entrees. Indeed, some dishes migrate back and forth between

> ## Hattie's
> 
> 111 St. Joseph St.
> Suttons Bay
> 616/271-6222
> 
> Appetizers $6 - $7
> Dinners generally $19-25
> Wines from $18 to $140
> (generally $19-35)

sections of the menu. One, which you'll find in this book, is grilled scallops. The very first time we dined at Hattie's we had them sauced with a sharp, white wine-based garlic butter and garnished with sage, chives and tiny nasturtiums. Times change, and Hattie's with them; today's grilled scallops are likely to be Thai style, served atop a cucumber relish with cilantro, jalapeño and lime juice.

The understatement at Hattie's extends even to Milliman's own description of it, which is "memorable dining in downtown Suttons Bay." Okay. And Monet was "a good artist from northern France."

Hattie's is one of Michigan's finest restaurants.

## Recipes

# Leelanau Country Inn

The first meal we ever had at John and Linda Sisson's Leelanau Country Inn, oddly enough, was a continental breakfast. It was some seven or eight years ago, and we had spent the night there while combining a weekend's bicycle outing with a visit with old friends. We still remember sitting in the summer-morning sunshine on the lawn looking out on quiet Little Traverse Lake, surrounded by Linda's magnificent flowers, and breakfasting on warm, buttery croissants and the freshest of fruit.

We decided that anyone who can make a continental breakfast that pleasant must be special, so we went back and had an equally memorable meal there that evening. A lot of other people must have thought the inn memorable, too, for the place was packed, and we were glad to have booked for dinner the moment we finished breakfast. It still is packed on busy summer evenings, and on Sundays, when the main event is brunch and you really want to arrive early.

The specialty at the inn is seafood. It arrives fresh daily, the saltwater variety flown in by a Boston supplier and the local fish from Carlson Market in Traverse City. The variety is staggering. One recent day's menu offered broiled whitefish, char-grilled mako shark, smoked haddock, broiled sole, sautéed scallops, broiled scrod, baked cod, fried soft-shell crab, steamed snow-crab legs, broiled bluefish and fried shrimp. Indeed, the inn has so much to offer that our first dinner there was memorable partly because of the time we spent deciding what to order. The appetizer list overflows with no less choice, from Cajun shrimp and Italian mussels to pan-fried alligator(!) and a Swiss onion soup the editors of Gourmet once saw fit to feature.

"We try to offer a little bit of every-thing," John explains. A bit of culinary legerdemain is required to transform this abundance into artful meals. John, who does most of the prep himself, relies on skillful mixing and matching of entrees with an array of such basic, tried-and-true sauces as lemon-butter, pecan-butter, and sherry-cream. He once told us that he found seven different uses for a certain Provençal sauce.

Interestingly, the inn has no chef, although one of the most valuable (and valued) players on a team of veteran employees is kitchen manager Matt Hill. The staff is stable and well versed. Regulars will tell you it includes the

Sissons' several family dogs, which frequently greet guests. They are such fixtures that winemaker Larry Mawby, who edited the Sissons' *Leelanau Country Inn Cookery*, has named wines after them (and one of dogs, Moira, is named for a Mawby wine).

The inn's cellar is a bit chauvinistic in that it contains almost nothing but Leelanau wines. The whites, in fact, are all local, from L. Mawby, Good Harbor, Boskydel, and Leelanau Ltd. The inn keeps one California Cab' on hand in case someone wants a nice red to go with prime rib.

The inn's thing with seafood traces, in large part, to John's start in restaurant management at one of the late Chuck Muer's Charley's Crab restaurants downstate. At 25 he was restaurant director of Detroit's Ponchartrain Hotel, and in 1980, faced with early burnout, he moved Up North. Here he met and married Linda, a Leland native.

In 1984 they bought what is now the Leelanau Country Inn. Built in 1890, it

---

## Leelanau Country Inn

149 E. Harbor Hwy. (M-22)
Maple City
616/228-5060

Dinners generally $16-22
(incl. potato/rice & veg.)
Appetizers typically $6-7
Wines $11-30

---

had been an inn since 1900 under one name or another, and it remains that now. It is as close as Northern Michigan gets to what the British would call a "Country House" hotel. That is, the restaurant is the main order of business and the six rooms upstairs are there just for an occasional diner who is also in need of lodging. Still, they are charming rooms, if you don't mind rural-cottage simplicity and the possibility of seasonal temperature extremes. And mornings still bring that lovely continental breakfast.

---

## Recipes

# Stubb's

One day last year, after a strenuous day of hiking the trails of Leelanau State Park and the shoreline of Cathead Bay, we stopped at Stubb's in Northport for what we thought was going to be a nice bowl of soup and a burger, and maybe some fries and slaw. That's what we'd had the last time we were there in 1992, and it had been pretty darn good. Were we ever surprised.

The place appeared pretty much the same—sort of a swept-up tavern with simple, tasteful furnishings. But the dinner we had bore about as much kinship to burgers and fries as Mozart does to, say, Hootie and the Blowfish. We feasted on walleye baked with a rich crust of basil-pistachio pesto, steamed, julienned vegetables and a discreet serving of the most interesting mashed potatoes in memory—half white potato, half yam, and abuzz with garlic. Not only was the food exceptional, the presentation was stunning. Imagine, we said to each other, all this in a place where we'd only been looking for a burger. By the time we had finished a delightful apple-crisp dessert and two cups of absolutely perfect coffee, we had recovered enough aplomb to venture into the kitchen and find out what on earth had happened to Stubb's.

The answer, we found out, is Darren Hawley. Almost before the ink dried on his diploma from the Culinary Institute, he and his family bought the Northport Bar. That was October, 1994, and they have been slowly transforming it ever since. Darren is the chef. His wife, Meghan, works the front, and Darren's parents, Joan and Bob Hawley, handle the books and the office work and generally hover helpfully and await instructions.

Darren may be young, but he is wise enough to realize that it takes time to make over a place like Stubb's. While offering inventive meals for adventuresome diners who want them, he doesn't ignore the old regulars who prefer things a bit simpler. "We do everything," he says. "We still do burgers, soup, pot pies, pasta dishes. We try to keep prices low, especially in the winter."

Pressed for a one-line description, he calls his style "peasant gourmet, a lot of simple dishes but very good." The dishes might be simple, but the ones we've enjoyed were presented with exquisite artistry. Darren obviously enjoys what he does and has fun in the kitchen.

Like most Northern Michigan restaurants, Stubb's changes character a bit with the seasons. Through the colder months, the stock in trade is beef—filet mignon, New York strips. In summer, however, Darren gets to do what he likes best, because the summer trade prefers lighter fare. "In summer," he says, "we try to push fresh seafood—salmon, walleye, whitefish."

Our guess is that if he keeps doing to it what he did to that walleye, he'll find himself pushing an awful lot of it. In a

| Stubb's |
|---|
| 115 S. Waukazoo St.<br>Northport<br>616/386-7611 |
| Dinners generally $14-18<br>Appetizers $3-6 |

town as small and remote as Northport, it's not easy keeping a restaurant going through long, northern winters, but if word gets around, people will find their way there just for Stubb's.

# Recipes

# God Bless Our Microclimate

Everyone associates Northern Michigan with cherries, but it is also wine country. The temperate microclimate that makes orchards productive works similar wonders for vineyards. In spring, the cold lake helps delay buds until frost is past, and in autumn the warm lake helps extend the season. It was more than 20 years ago when Bernie Rink, the librarian at Northwestern Michigan College, began harvesting grapes on his farm near Lake Leelanau, proving it possible to produce wine Up North. The loquacious Rink, now retired from the college, still regales visitors at his Boskydel Vineyard. Every afternoon but Christmas he has wine to taste and yarns to spin. *Boskydel, 7501 E. Otto Rd., Lake Leelanau. 616/256-7272.*

Leelanau's other wineries also welcome visitors. L. Mawby Vineyards' tasting room is open Thursday, Friday and Saturday afternoons from May into October. Leelanau's smallest winery, it is also widely regarded as tops. Larry Mawby once told us he doesn't want to grow more grapes, so the only way to increase profits is to make better wine. Local oenophiles delight in his dry vignoles and his fine sparkling white. *L. Mawby Vineyards, 4519 Elm Valley Rd., Suttons Bay. 616/271-3522.*

Leelanau Cellars Ltd. has also been producing interesting wine since the 1970s, including their popular "Tall Ship" Chardonnay and a trio of blended, semi-dry wines named for summer, winter and spring. Tasters are welcome every afternoon, and for hourly tours in summer. *Leelanau Wine Cellars Ltd., 12693 Tatch Rd., Omena. 616/386-5201.*

Good Harbor Vineyards and Winery offers daily tours and tastings June through October. Semi-dry "Trillium" blend and Chardonnay are local favorites, and "Fishtown White" is a fine value. Tasting room is on M-22 three miles south of Leland, adjacent to Manitou Market. *Good Harbor Vineyards and Winery, 2191 S. Manitou Trail, Leland. 616/256-7165.*

# Other Seasons Other Reasons

This extraordinarily scenic part of Michigan has a number of interesting eateries that are not all wine, roses, white tablecloths and candlelight. They, too, enjoy loyal followings for other very good reasons. This was resort country long before the area began going cosmopolitan on us, and some of the restaurants go back to a time when things were a bit simpler. Some brand new ones, on the other hand, have appeared precisely because of the changes, catering to a clientele increasingly keen on extraordinary food even in the simplest of surroundings.

We spend a lot of time in Leelanau, summer and winter—cycling, skiing, beachcombing, hiking. It's a grand place to mix outdoor adventure with lovely scenery and good food. Very often, a day's exercise leaves us with a powerful hunger but disinclined to inflict our tousled appearance, windblown hair and scruffy moccasins on refined ladies and gents out for a romantic evening over candlelight. That's when we feel thoroughly comfortable at one of those delightful pubs where the food is as good as the atmosphere is casual.

Then, too, there are some awfully good seasonal establishments here, including some of our real favorites. A few of them close because they are in charming old buildings that don't have heat; some close because there just isn't enough year-round business.

## The Mysterious Manitous

The Manitou Islands seem to hover on the horizon wherever you go in Leelanau. How can any adventurer resist finding out what's out there? The ferry leaves each morning (in season) from Leland's Fishtown, crosses to South Manitou in about 90 minutes, and returns in late afternoon. Pack a lunch and hike the island's miles of trails, or just visit the old Coast Guard life-saving station and lighthouse. The world's largest white cedar tree grows on the island, as does one of the biggest yellow birches. From the southwestern shore, you can see the wreck of a freighter that foundered in a storm decades ago. Two or three times a week a ferry calls at North Manitou as well, for adventuresome backpacking campers. To check schedules and fares to either island, call the Manitou Ferry at 616/256-9061. Check, too, with the Leelanau Conservancy (616/256-9665) to see if you might be able to join one of their expert-guided, day-long, nature hikes on South Manitou (or somewhere else in this interesting county).

Whatever the reason, when they are open, we enjoy them very much, and when they are not, we have learned to wait patiently.

## Cappuccino's

For all the adventure available Up North, one of the nicest things to do outdoors is lunch at Cappuccino's on a summer day when proprietor John Dozier has brought in a chamber quartet to play for al fresco diners in the parking lot. In seasons when not even the hardiest foodie wants to sit outside in Suttons Bay, Dozier sometimes invites celebrity chefs to show off their amateur skills in the kitchen. It takes creativity like this to keep a good restaurant going through long, northern winters, but there has to be food to match. Cappuccino's has that, too. Dozier started small about four years ago, offering coffee, pastries and a limited variety of deli-lunch items that you were welcome to eat on the premises if you could find one of the eight or ten seats vacant. It says a lot for his food that he has had to expand twice already, and still the clientele spills over when it can to tables outside. From breakfast onwards, Dozier provides an array of freewheeling soups, sandwiches, salads and pastas. This food is not just interesting, it has scale. His aptly named "Viking Breakfast" requires three eggs, half a pound of ham and turkey, a hunk of butter

and two slices of Swiss. Some of the dishes have names as long as the waiting line on a busy Sunday in July. Try "Royal British Blue Stilton Cream of Vidalia Onion Soup." Once you've learned to say it, turn to our recipe section and try making it. If you don't want all five gallons his recipe produces, just stop by Cappuccino's. John will be happy to sell you some, one bowl at a time, and if you're lucky, he'll throw in a little Vivaldi. *Cappuccino's, 102 N. Broadway, Suttons Bay. 616/271-2233.*

## Hose House Deli

It's hard to pin down exactly what kind of place this is, although there's no doubt that it is good and that it is Greek. Sam Secson, the owner, chef and chief bottle-washer, does some knockout dishes, from lamb stew to a Greek pizza that won big at last year's pizza convention. (We'll bet you didn't even know there was a pizza convention, much less that it's in Las Vegas every year, and that the judges from *Pizza Today* magazine judged Sam Secson's Greek Pizza the nation's very best "exotic pizza.") The dish is his stock in trade at the Hose House, but we have to tell you he does some

other things that are every bit as good, and some of it hardly classifies as deli food. The first time we ever went there we had moussaka and lamb stew that were too good to be believed. Sam has shared his prize-winning Greek pizza recipe with us, and his recipe for lamb stew. But don't even ask about the moussaka. "Family recipe," he told us. "Ancient Greek secret. Sorry." You'll just have to do what we do when we get a hunger for it: Go to Suttons Bay and beg him to make it. The Hose House is a charming little place that gets a lot of mileage out of a tiny old fire barn. The kitchen is right behind the deli counter, and up front are some tables and benches for those of us who don't even want deli food to take out. Through summer Sam has the doors open every day from 8 a.m. until 9 p.m., but he keeps a somewhat saner pace the rest of the time by not opening until lunchtime and by closing altogether on Sunday and Monday. In the dead of winter he sometimes closes altogether to rest up for the pizza convention.
*Hose House Deli, 303 St. Joseph St., Suttons Bay. 616/271-6303.*

## Fischer's Happy Hour

Talk to any food-lover who has spent much time in Leelanau and sooner or later you'll hear about the burgers at Fischer's. This old-time, family-operated

---

## Away from the Crowd I

There's nothing like a romantic picnic for two on a remote beach, and do we have the place. Stop first at the Manitou Market on M-22 south of Leland for some fresh berries or fruit, then go next door to Good Harbor Winery and pick up a bottle of their Chardonnay for the cooler. Then swing by the deli counter at the Leland Mercantile for some cheese to go with the fruit. Now find your way to Leelanau State Park up north of Northport, and from the trailhead off Densmore Road follow the markers to the seldom-used beach. Even if someone else is there, you can get lost among the dunes. It's winter, you say? So ski in. The trails swoop and soar through and over peaceful, scenic, forested dunes, and you'll find the shoreline even more secluded then.

---

roadhouse on M-22 between Northport and Leland is known all over Northern Michigan for burgers and homemade soup. The secret to the burgers, you'll discover on your first visit, is attention to detail. It starts with good beef, which is then done as you ask, smothered in grilled onions, buried under the smoothest cheese, and served on ample buns with the freshest of lettuce, tomato, pickle and whatever else you choose from the list of options. From the road, Fischer's resembles a white cottage with a glassed-in porch, but inside there's no mistaking the tavern, where a pool table sits at one end of the friendly, pine-paneled, north-woods barroom. The bar sits at the other, and well-worn tables fill the gap. In back is a dining room that's only slightly less casual. Fischer's is the perfect place to start recouping all the calories you'll lose on a long afternoon of skiing the cross-country trails at Leelanau State Park or cycling around the tip of Leelanau. *Fischer's Happy Hour, 7144 N. Manitou Trail W., Northport. 616/386-9923.*

## Western Avenue Grill

This place is sort of like the girl next door. Once aptly named "The Soda Shop," it is now all grown up, offering rather more sophisticated fare, a drink or a glass of wine if you wish, and even a little live music once in a while. The grill is a bright spot among the artsy shops on the main drag in Glen Arbor that does breakfast, lunch and dinner. It is a very satisfying stop to stoke up for a winter's day of skiing in the National Lakeshore, or to unwind with an early supper after a long August bike ride around Glen Lake. One outdoornik friend of ours who enjoys hiking the national Lakeshore, Dave Taylor, is a connoisseur of home-made meat loaf, and he considers the Grill's awesome. He and Lisa (she prefers whitefish, dusted with Parmesan) stop there regularly en route to and from their frolics among the dunes. Like the girl next door, the Western Avenue Grill is every bit as wholesome,

straightforward and unpretentious as when it was a soda shop, but much more interesting. *Western Avenue Grill, 6410 Western Ave., Glen Arbor. 616/334-3362.*

## Cafe Bliss

This is just the place for vegetarians weary of settling for the lone dish so many restaurants tack onto the menu as a sort of afterthought for diners who'd rather not have meat. It's a quiet, subdued place in a simple house on Suttons Bay's main street with food as light and gentle as the atmosphere. The omelets, salads, and other light fare come in imaginative combinations, and exquisitely presented. Cafe Bliss is meatless, but fish of some sort is always on the menu, says co-owner Sara Johnson, and most of the time, chicken as well. Sara opened the restaurant in 1994 with her brother, T. J. Johnson, and his wife, Ewa Einhorn. Sara had done catering and run the deli at Traverse City's Oryana Food Co-op, and T.J. and Ewa were just back from New York, where they'd worked at the Russian Tea Room. In just a couple of summers at Cafe Bliss, they've crafted some delicious evidence to show that "healthy" cuisine doesn't have to be bland, dull, or homely, but can be downright stimulating, be it breakfast, lunch or dinner. Consider "Linguine Brasilia," in which sun-dried tomatoes and a variety of mushrooms come on a bed of pasta in a creamy garlic sauce. Or a sesame-veggie pasta with stir-fried, marinated tofu and a spicy peanut sauce. Fish and fowl include such delights as roasted whitefish and pan-fried walleye, Cajun grilled-chicken salad or a stir-fry of chicken marinated in garlic, orange zest and ginger with grilled veggies on brown rice. Cafe Bliss closes in winter so Sara, T.J. and Ewa can get some rest. *Cafe Bliss, 420 St. Joseph St., Suttons Bay. 616/271-5000.*

## Edible Events

Face it, the folks in Leelanau County know how to celebrate food. You could spend an entire summer celebrating it with them, especially in Northport. Northporters kick off the culinary year with their Smelt Supper each May at the fire hall. They take time out to attend the annual Food and Wine Festival in Leland in June, but hurry home for the Northport Wine Festival in August (unless the National Coho Salmon Festival in Honor is too tempting). In September the folks in Northport have their annual Fish Boil at the town park, and there's a Fly-In Pancake Breakfast at the airport. Leelanau County's civic food year winds down in October at the Glen Arbor Women's Club Smorgasbord.

## Northern Delights

Northern Delights started life as a "whole-grain organic bakery" more than a decade ago, behind a storefront in tiny Benzonia. The bakery became a bakery-and-deli the next year, still with the same organic, natural style, and it was the right thing at the right time and in the right place. Over the next few years they added tables and began serving breakfasts and lunches, and then Jim Barnes showed up. Barnes is one of those fortunates who get degrees in philosophy (his from Ohio's Miami University) then go to work doing what they really want. What he really wanted was to cook. After apprenticing under chefs in California, he visited his parents at their cottage on Crystal Lake in 1988 and took a dishwashing job at Northern Delights. Six months later, the owner decided to sell, and Jim joined four partners in buying. He added a dinner menu and found a ready market in Benzonia for his simple, natural and heavily vegetarian fare. The market was even more ready after the advent of a wine list a few years ago helped him shed the "health-food" image. This is still a doggedly healthy restaurant, however, with a menu that is neither long nor complicated. Barnes calls it "a natural restaurant specializing in ethnic foods." The emphasis is on food of the Middle East, which he considers healthiest of all "because of its grains, vegetables, and high-protein, non-dairy ingredients." Here you'll find baba ganouj and tahini, hummus and tabbouleh, as well as more traditional Northern Michigan recipes, such as walleye sprinkled with dill and baked. Fish is always on the menu, chicken makes frequent appearances, and the vegetarian will always feel thoroughly at home, be it time for breakfast, lunch, dinner, or Sunday brunch. Benzonia is a very small place, so Northern Delights shuts down in winter, making up for it in warmer times with occasional live music—jazz, blues and bluegrass. *Northern Delights, 1058 Michigan Ave. (US-31), Benzonia. 616/882-9631.*

## The Cove

In a land of spectacular views, the one from the Cove in Leland is unique, looking down on picturesque Fishtown and out over Lake Michigan and the Manitous. You can almost envision the days when real fishermen aboard the *Ace, Etta, Nu Deal* and *Bonnie Lass* came and went under flocks of raucous gulls. From tables by the windows, you sometimes see salmon leaping up the spillway in their reproductive frenzy. The menu is direct and basic: seafood, steaks, ribs, chicken, and the obligatory whitefish, which comes fried, broiled, almondine or Cajun-style. In the house specialty, "Fishtown Stew," whitefish, mussels, shrimp and scallops swim in a tangy tomato sauce. The Cove kicks off its season by celebrating the return of summer sunshine over Memorial Day. *The Cove, 111 River St., Leland. 616/256-9834.*

## Riverside Inn

We confess to a really soft spot in our hearts for the Riverside Inn. One of us (obviously the older) remembers staying there in the 1940s when innkeeper Blanche Swartz would cheerfully make breakfast from any bluegills her young guest caught. The place

has gone through various incarnations since, and we rediscovered it in the 1980s when a former owner was turning out French food in the big, old kitchen. We were delighted to find we could not only dine there, but stay there. New owner Clayton Weeks's less pricey, bistro-style menu is accented by Thai and Southwestern themes. Unchanged is the charm of the dining room, on a pine-paneled porch that didn't even exist in Blanche's day. The original dining room is now a sort of tavern-in-the-round, with 360 degrees of bar and elbow room all around for the clientele. For nice weather, there's a lovely deck in back from which to gaze across the river at the town library, which is on the site where Blanche's brother Jake had his boat business. Although closed in winter, the Riverside is one of our favorites in season, for both nostalgia and dining. *Riverside Inn, 302 E. River St., Leland. 616/256-9971.*

# What Is This "Regional Cuisine," Anyway?

Talk very long with a chef in Northern Michigan and sooner or later you'll hear the term "regional cuisine." Restaurants Up North have been using the term to describe their style ever since Wes Westhoven introduced the idea a quarter century ago at The Rowe. It's a practice borrowed from Europe, which hasn't traditionally had the pervasive food-distribution industry that so homogenizes American restaurant food. European chefs rely more on what they can buy from local farms and markets, and their menus reflect distinctive local variations. Where olives grow, they use olive oil; where mushrooms appear, they use mushrooms. In Northern Michigan, then, "regional" means maple syrup trapped from the trees in March, wild leeks or ramps that appear on forest floors in April, asparagus that sends up tender new shoots in May, strawberries in June, blueberries in July, raspberries and blackberries in August. We have perch, walleye, trout, and salmon. Above all, we have whitefish. Naturally, cherries figure heavily in Northern Michigan regional cooking, as do apples and the other fruits grown in the region. Squashes have been staples since Indian days, as have pheasant, duck, and venison. One historical account of a Mackinac Islanders' sugar camp tells of "partridge and goose kept frozen from the fall hunt, and bears paws and beaver tails and stuffed rabbit roasted whole at the end of long sticks." Much "regional" food is now regional only in a historical sense, being brought in from afar nowadays by those food distributors. Perch, trout and walleye are farm-raised, and even the salmon from Lake Michigan got there only because they were planted. Nonetheless, the region's best chefs buy fresh fruits, vegetables, meat and fish from local producers as often as possible, and spend a lot of time haggling at the kitchen door with neighbors selling fish, herbs, morels, sprouts, asparagus, watercress and fruit.

## Hot Ticket in Cedar

If you love the graceful lines and varnished gentility of old Chris Crafts, Gar Woods and Old Towns, don't miss the annual Classic Boat Rendezvous each June in Suttons Bay. Those boats have polish. But if what you want is Polish, then try tiny Cedar's mammoth event, the Polka Fest in June. Do a little dancing, have a little fun and games, and maybe sip a brewski or two. If the spirit moves you, you can even go to a Polka Mass on Sunday. For food-lovers, the hot ticket in Cedar is Pleva's Meats, which is where Ray Pleva invented and, of course, sells his famous (as seen on TV!) meat-and-cherries product, Plevalean. *Pleva's Meats, 8974 Kasson, Cedar. 616/228-5000.*

seriously a few years ago after a company he worked for in Phoenix folded. He moved to Leland in the early '90s with his wife, Ellen (whose sister just happens to be Chez Panisse's Alice Watters), and went into the business in 1995 using sourdough he made on his back porch and flour from a Mennonite co-op in Kansas. Twice—1994 and '96—his bread won the *Coupe du Monde* bake-off in Paris. He also makes a classic, sweet, French baguette. You'll find his breads at outlets in Leland, Northport, Omena, Suttons Bay, and Traverse City. *Stonehouse Bread, 407 S. Main, Leland. 616/256-2577.*

At John Hoyt's Leelanau Cheese Company, in an old garage by the Harbor Bar tavern in Omena, cheesemaking is a sort of spectator sport. You can watch them make their Boursin-like spreads—plain, garlic-flavored, or with herbs from Woodland Farm near Northport. *Leelanau Cheese Co., Omena, 616/386-7731; Woodland Herbs, 7741 N. Manitou Trail. 616/386-5081.*

## Resources

Northern Michigan food-lovers rave about the sourdough breads produced by former newsman Bob Pisor at his Stonehouse Bakery in Leland. Long a hobby breadmaker, Pisor took it up

## Recipes

# Traverse City

Traverse City may be Northern Michigan's center of population, commerce and culture, but even in the heart of the city you're in the great outdoors. Fishermen cast for steelhead within view of rush-hour traffic, there are scenic beaches right downtown, and skiers enjoy backwoods trails within minutes of Front and Cass streets. It's all part of the charm of living in the place we lovingly call TC—a lively, sophisticated city yet still closely surrounded by orchards, farms, vineyards and forests.

The town is especially alive in summer, with water sports, nightlife, and throngs of visitors. You can enjoy a day-cruise on a tall ship, go windsurfing, parasailing or deep-water trolling. Live music is everywhere, and headliners appear weekly at nearby Interlochen. Increasingly, however, this is a year-round place, with jazz and blues to liven up long winter nights, monthly pops and classical concerts by the Traverse Symphony, as well as professional dance and lively community theater. The museum at the local college has a fine permanent collection of Inuit art, and on the waterfront an authentic replica of an 18th-century Great Lakes schooner, the *Madeline*, serves as a floating history lesson.

Proud of the lumber-town past, Traverse Citians have lovingly restored whole neighborhoods of brick-paved streets and stately Victorian homes.

They're just the place for a stroll after dinner on a summer's eve before a nightcap and some after-hours jazz.

Lodging, of course, is abundant, and ranges from rustic cabins to luxury resorts. But if you really want something different, try a cabin on the schooner *Malabar*. She cruises the bay by day, then at night becomes a floating B&B.

To get the most out of the grand restaurants we're sending you to, you have to burn off calories first, and this is certainly the place for it. Try a fast 10k ski on the Vasa trail, or cycle the back roads through Old Mission Peninsula's neatly groomed orchards and vineyards. In a place like Traverse City, it's a cinch to enjoy a creamy Stroganoff with a clear conscience.

# Bowers Harbor Inn

Dining at Bowers Harbor is like visiting an interesting old friend who lives in a stately country manor, except that pastoral countryside has been replaced by a stunning view of Grand Traverse Bay through a grove of soaring pines. Moreover, the friend you're visiting is a ghost.

The restaurant, in fact, once was a stately manor, built in the 1880s as a summer place by a Chicago lumber baron named Stickney. His wife, Genevieve, made delicious fruit brandy, but she was somewhat eccentric, and she buried her brandy bottles in the yard. Some are whispered to be there still. When Genevieve took ill, Stickney hired a nurse, who soon became his mistress. Then the old goat died, leaving his fortune to the nurse and nothing but the house to poor Genevieve. There, in despair, she hanged herself. Now she is said to go about after hours slamming doors, dousing lamps, breaking mirrors, tearing paintings from the walls, and moving furniture around.

We hope you'll not let all this keep you away, however. Ghosts aside, it's a fine mealtime adventure and on some nights you can enjoy haunting dinner music by John Wunsch, an accomplished classical guitarist from the neighborhood.

Bowers Harbor, ghost and all, is owned by veteran Michigan restaurateur Howard Schelde, who also lives in the neighborhood, and run by manager Randy Sharp. Sharp refers to Bowers Harbor as "classic fine dining with new American influences," which, he explains, is another way of saying, "We walk the line between pleasing the traditionalist and the adventurer."

That's why, on Bowers Harbor's menu, you'll find such old stand-bys as beef and whitefish, bearnaise and hollandaise, lamb chops and oysters Rockefeller, listed alongside such decidedly non-trad surprises as rattlesnake bean gumbo and egg rolls stuffed with ancho chilis. "We're a melting pot," says Sharp. "Pan-Pacific, Southwestern . . . . If it's available, we'll use it." Part of the adventure of Bowers Harbor is the game that often appears on the menu: venison, pheasant, duck, salmon. "We think," says Sharp, "that we should offer things people do not often cook at home."

It is his view that "fine

dining should be a feast in three ways: for the eyes, the palate and the memory. This is a special-occasion restaurant."

Bowers' menu always includes a dish called "fish-in-a-bag," in which roughy, crabmeat, lobster and shrimp are presented with a wine sauce *en papillotte.* Because it is so frequently requested by customers, Sharp says, "It will be there until the building burns down." Frankly, we prefer their pecan-coated walleye with hazelnut cream sauce, although they also do a fine Norwegian salmon with a piquant apricot glaze. Perhaps our most memorable meal there consisted of dainty medallions of duckling in a red-currant sauce following an appetizer of Brie, pecan and cranberry baked in a puff-pastry purse. It was memorable because it was beautifully prepared and presented and impeccably served on a snowy Tuesday in November when we appeared to be the only diners present. On a night like that, when lesser restaurants might

<table>
<tr><td colspan="2">Bowers Harbor Inn</td></tr>
<tr><td colspan="2">13512 Peninsula Dr.<br>Traverse City<br>616/223-4222</td></tr>
<tr><td colspan="2">Appetizers generally $5-7<br>Entrees typically $20-25<br>Desserts $4-5<br>Off-season "Hearthstone Dinners"<br>  for $18</td></tr>
</table>

let down, such a performance said much about standards and consistency.

Howard Schelde displays neighborhood loyalty by featuring wines produced nearby at Château Chantal, Château Grand Traverse, and Bowers Harbor Vineyards. The latter's grapes grow right outside the restaurant, and we can't help wondering if their quality is influenced in any way by all that brandy buried out there.

## Recipes

# La Cuisine Amical

The name means "friendly kitchen," and that's certainly appropriate. Since it opened a couple of years ago, this kitchen has made friends of every food-lover Up North with charm, cuisine and a versatility that borders on all things to all people. From the very beginning, La Cuisine Amical has been part pâtisserie, part coffee house, part sidewalk cafe. And now, with the addition of a beer and wine list and evening table service, it has matured into a full-scale restaurant that promises to be one of Northern Michigan's best.

You can eat in or carry out, and you can go there for breakfast, lunch or dinner. The kitchen is so friendly it is right there as you enter, behind display racks of freshly made baguettes, croissants, eclairs, tarts and cookies. In the morning, there are fresh fruits, croissants and glorious Starbucks coffees. By late morning, tempting French-style cafe meals are prepared before your very eyes. Poultry and meats roast on spits alongside bowls heaped with the freshest of salads, including a simple, low-fat Caesar that is one of the best anywhere. There are quiches and pochettes, and pizzettas and pot pies hot from the oven. You'll find interesting soups and bisques, including a daily pot of basil-tomato bisque that deserves to be enshrined.

There is no dearth of ambience even at breakfast and lunch, when the service is cafeteria-style. The simple, old-brick walls are adorned only by a few, lovely, oil canvases in ornate frames. A cozy, three-sided fireplace is flanked by tables that are perfect for intimate conversations on snowy winter days or romantic murmurings by candlelight on soft summer nights.

Out front is a sidewalk cafe where you can linger over lunch on summer afternoons and watch the colorful parade of shoppers and tourists on Front Street, or spend an hour trading gossip over cappuccino.

The tables are sheltered from the elements and bathed in warm air from overhead heaters, so you can still eat al fresco in the chilly weather we sometimes have Up North.

Even without wine and table service, La Cuisine Amical became one of Northern Michigan's most popular spots in just a couple of years. Now it should positively soar. As we go to press, Chef Dave Denison has not fully written the evening table-service menu, but he promises more of the same sort of simple, bistro fare with which he has already captured so many food-lovers' hearts. That means you will probably enjoy even more variety of his savory *rôtis* of lamb and chicken, pot pies, soups and salads, breads and pastries. And, he says, even by evening you will still be able to enjoy the convenience of counter service.

## La Cuisine Amical

229 E. Front Street
Traverse City
616/941-8888

Soup and salad lunches $5-7
Pot pies, pizzettas, quiches $3-7
Dinners generally $8-12

One day, if all goes well, the former State Theater next door may be refurbished as a performing arts center for stage productions and concerts. When that happens, La Cuisine Amical will be the perfect spot for dinner before or after the show. Even now, however, no visit to Traverse City is complete without at least one meal there.

## Recipes

# Old Mission Tavern

If your next trip to Old Mission Tavern is your first, you won't believe us when we tell you the place once was a Dairy Freeze. That was in 1980, however, and the tavern has undergone more than a few changes. All are changes for the better, of course, and today the OMT has evolved into a fine roadside tavern and restaurant that is also a sort of art colony.

The proprietress, Verna Bartnick, is a sculptor, whose works of wood, bronze and welded metals adorn several local landmarks. She moved to the site of the restaurant in 1976 and set up a studio, which is still next door. The restaurant sort of evolved, starting with that Dairy Freeze which helped Verna avoid becoming one of those starving artists you're always hearing about. It obviously worked, and today's establishment is a somewhat better restaurant-cum-art gallery that displays the work of artists from near and far.

The food has artistic merit on its own, especially if you like a rich palette. Butter, cream, and cheese figure heavily in the scheme of things at the

Old Mission Tavern, and the kitchen turns out some very full-flavored fare. As you might expect of a place with an artist in charge, much about the OMT has a decidedly creative flair, expressed in European accents with a rural inflection. The tavern offers some incredibly hearty soups and stews which, with a salad, would satisfy a trencherman all by themselves. Poached salmon with shrimp and scallops in champagne butter is chef Frank Lyon's favorite, but Verna will probably suggest artichoke chicken, a dish of butter-sautéed breasts covered with a white wine and cream sauce that's laced with scallions, shiitake mushrooms and garlic. It is one of Verna's lighter dishes, after the pasta Rufino and vegetarian stir-fry she always seems to have available for the calorie-impaired.

The last time we were there, we were chatting with Verna about art and food and stuff, and she got to telling us about a new dish on her menu called "Blue Cheese Spinach Pasta with Bacon." Next thing we knew she had a sample in front of us. Well, we assure you that the name barely hints at the content, which you'll see from the recipe later in this book

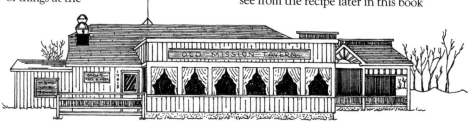

includes not just blue cheese, pasta and bacon, but Parmesan and mozzarella and the sourdough bread it comes with. Frankly, it's delicious, but I'd not want you telling my cardiologist I said that.

Ambiencewise, there's a bit of something for everyone at the OMT. The gallery in back (formally the "Bella Galleria") doubles as a banquet room, but most of the time is nice for a little browsing and intellectual conversation over cocktails or an after-dinner drink. The main room (the "tavern" part) is a sort of neighborhood watering hole where you're likely to find a some local regulars sharing an inside joke. Adjoining that is a bright sun porch where romantically inclined diners can enjoy seclusion.

In typical European fashion, the tavern is a family business. Verna, the busy *Maman*, greets guests and oversees staff, while her son tends bar. Her husband, Arthur, a retired teacher and salesman, looks after the building and

## Old Mission Tavern

17015 Center Rd.
Old Mission
616/223-7280

Appetizers about $5
Entrees generally $12-13
Most wines $18-25

grounds. Since Old Mission Peninsula is home to several wineries (four at last count), the tavern features their products on its list, much as the *fermes auberges* of the French countryside do the output of the neighborhood *vignobles*.

This is a grand place to start and end a long autumn bike tour among the orchards and vineyards and lovely scenic views of Old Mission Peninsula. But ride really hard, so you can enjoy the food in good conscience.

## Recipes

# Paparazzi

This is not your basic Italian restaurant with red and white checkered tablecloths and candles in old Chianti bottles. While hardly stiff and formal, either, it is a bit more up-scale. Yes, Luigi, you can get spaghetti and meatballs if you insist, but why would you? For just another few thousand lire you can have a marvelous dish of linguine with *frutti di mare* swimming in a white wine sauce, or pheasant-stuffed raviolis in a wild mushroom sauce. Paparazzi is a delightful little restaurant, tucked away in a corridor off the lobby of the Grand Traverse Resort—quiet, refined, intimate. The menu is not extensive, but what they do they do well, and the service matches the standards throughout the resort—that is to say, excellent. In keeping with its name, the restaurant originally was decorated by scores of framed, candid photos of celebrities and restaurant patrons. These vanished in a recent remodeling, which is fine with us. Who wants to dine under the gaze of a hundred strangers? Besides, the era of the *paparazzo* sort of passed away with Jackie O, didn't it? Now, we understand, not only the name but the very restaurant itself are destined to disappear in a year or so in yet another overhaul of the resort's outlets.

Meanwhile, in its present form, Paparazzi provides a delightful evening out. We are particularly fond of two dishes which we enjoy not because they are particularly fancy, but because they are simple and classic. One is chicken piccata, alive with the happy sting of lemon and capers; the other is veal Marsala, whose mushroom-laced sauce is neither soupy thin nor overly rich. The appetizer list beckons grazers, although it's not a list for the light eater. For the determined pizza-eater, Paparazzi has individual pies with a variety of toppings, from all the usual to such novelties as Gorgonzola, pesto and roast garlic. Obviously, we can only speculate about this restaurant in its future form,

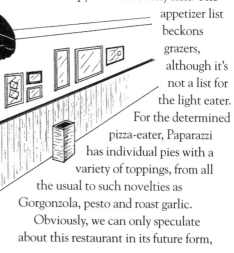

which is likely to include an altogether different name. From what intelligence we have collected, however, we gather it will continue to offer interesting fare with a sort of Italian flair, although perhaps in more casual and spacious surroundings whose focus, we hear, may be an open-fire brick oven. We have little doubt, given what we know of the resort's commitment to good food and service, that it, too, will be a fine restaurant.

Whatever the folks at the resort do to what is now Paparazzi, there's one thing we hope they leave as-is, because we do not want to be left without its bright tomato-sauce flavors, alive with cheerful

Mediterranean herbs and cushioned by a creamy-soft texture. They call it lasagna, but we call it heaven.

## Paparazzi

Grand Traverse Resort
6300 US-31 N.
Traverse City
616/938-2100

Appetizers  $6-7
Pasta dishes $13-15
Dinners generally $14-18
    (incl. salad, veg, potato)

## Recipes

# Poppycock's

This spot on Traverse City's Front Street has been a restaurant of one sort or another throughout living memory, but never has there been anything there quite like Poppycock's. In the old days (the really old days) it was a counter-booths-and-jukebox kind of family place called "Pete's," whose motto was "the fish you eat today slept last night in Grand Traverse Bay." Some of the original, black-white-and-chrome pre-WWII decor remains, but Pete Batsakis probably wouldn't recognize the food that comes from the kitchen, for it is distinctively '90s.

The owners, Mark and Josie Butzier, brought the name "Poppycock's" with them when they moved to Traverse City from Aspen, where their original Poppycock's was an eight-seat, lunch-counter crêperie. When Aspen got too pricey in the rip-roaring '80s, the two Michigan natives decided to head back home to a kinder, gentler place. Aspen's loss was Traverse City's gain.

Locals and visitors alike greeted Poppycock's with enthusiasm. Within a few months it had become a Traverse City lunch-time favorite for its delightfully imaginative salads, pastas and sandwiches, incorporating such interesting stuff as sprouts, nuts, fresh fruits and veggies, avocado, red onion, cucumber, mustard, and tangy dressings. With the addition in the early '90s of a drinks and wine license Poppycock's blossomed as a fine dinner restaurant as well. By day, the fare is still built around the same delightful recipes (largely Josie's) that came east from Aspen. The salads—meals by themselves in which the whole food pyramid is represented—are as delightfully named as they are designed; "Screaming Chicken Salad," for instance, blends chicken on greens with apples, tarragon,

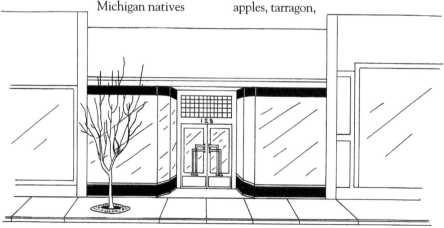

bacon, nuts and a light vinaigrette. Pastas include the usual tomato-sauced entries, laced with fresh herbs and garlic, cheese and pine nuts, as well as such non-trad dishes as grilled chicken and broccoli with a mustard-Brie sauce.

The salads and pasta dishes remain after dark, but the rest of the menu changes into somewhat more formal and sophisticated dress. That's when you'll find whitefish in a peppercorn crust garnished with fresh fruit and a kiwi-vinaigrette sauce, or grilled duck breast with a blueberry-port wine sauce and a garnish of wild rice and steamed baby carrots. Perhaps the fish didn't sleep last night in Grand Traverse Bay, but then old Pete never offered pan-seared salmon under a ragout of leeks, garlic and mushroom (a Poppycock's favorite for which you'll find the recipe in this book).

Poppycock's is a haven for the vegetarian, with a list of five or six dishes to choose from. There are ratatouille raviolis, for instance, and grilled pizzettas with feta, mushrooms, black olives and sun-dried tomatoes. There are quesadillas of lentils and creamy fontina cheese, with onion, tomato, salsa and cilantro-lime sour cream. Why, veg dishes like these tempt the carnivores, too.

---

## Poppycock's

128 E. Front Street
Traverse City
616/941-7632

Luncheon
Salads, pastas about $6
Sandwiches $5-6

Evening
Dinners $12-13
Pasta dinners about $8
Dinner salads about $6
Appetizers about $5.50
Wines generally $13-25

---

Lunch is still the busiest time at Poppycock's, and even on the deadest midwinter workdays the seats fill at rush hour. But the workday rush in Northern Michigan is short, and you can avoid a long wait by arriving a few minutes either side of it. In summer, however, when the fudgies flock to Front Street, you can expect to queue up and have a few minutes to read the day's specials on the chalkboard by the door and admire the funky decor which is a sort of perpetual work-in-progress.

## Recipe

# Reflections

To our way of thinking, Reflections would be worth frequent visits regardless of food, because of owner Ralph Bergsma's wholehearted support of the arts. A big-band fan, he throws a "Spring Swing" fund-raiser each June for the Traverse Symphony that goes a long way to keeping Beethoven and Mozart alive and well Up North. Whenever someone says "thanks" in public, he does one of those aw-shucks numbers and ducks back into the crowd. To the point here, while we certainly hope you'll support folks who support the arts, we also think you'll like Reflections for its stylish fare and the expansive view of East Bay it affords you from the fourth-floor roof of the Waterfront Inn.

Under Ralph's son, Kirk, the restaurant recently underwent some simplification. Servers exchanged starched white shirts in favor of short-sleeved blue. Tablecloths vanished. Entree-sized salads appeared on the menu, along with an expanded list of appetizers. Sandwiches and pastas also materialized, alongside such standbys as prime rib, filet mignon, rack of lamb and planked whitefish. Atop the menu now are a burger and a sourdough chicken club (in good Up North style, it has a layer of Swiss). These are closely followed by pastas, including one in which prosciutto, pepperoncini, sun-dried tomatoes, and garlic are cooked in wine and oil and tossed with linguine. Fancy fare notwithstanding, these, too, are arts worth supporting.

Seafood has always been a strength at Reflections, and remains so. Whitefish, naturally, figures prominently in the game plan, as do steamed crab, pan-fried walleye and salmon, and char-grilled swordfish. Shrimp appear sautéed in oil with garlic, shallots, wine and basil over a vegetable rice. Typical of the new regime, perhaps, is a dish of charbroiled chicken breasts sauced with a sweet-sour apple-cherry chutney. It's so healthful you can guiltlessly precede it with a cup of Reflections' sinfully thick chowder of smoked shrimp, corn and rice.

The salad and appetizer lists encourage grazing. The menu sports six salads— which come with bread—and 10 appetizers, ranging from shrimp cocktail and stuffed mushrooms to sushi and tapas. Consider making dinner of a cup of chowder, a Niçoise salad of grilled swordfish, tomato, artichoke, black olives, pepperoncini and capers, and a sushi platter with smoked eel. (Although, quite frankly, we like the appetizer in which crab and wild rice cakes come in a pool of stone-ground mustard sauce.)

Unchanged, happy to say, is Reflections' custom of popping a little heart on its menu next to dishes that are good for the ticker by reason of low fat or cholesterol or whatever.

## Reflections

Waterfront Inn, 2061 US-31 N
Traverse City
616/938-2321

Dinners generally $14-16
  (includes soup or salad)
Sandwiches  $7-8.50
Pastas about $8
Appetizers about $5
Salads $6.25-9.50

One of the nicest things about the Waterfront is, well, the waterfront. The restaurant's fourth-floor vantage point provides sweeping perspective up East Bay, but it is not so lofty that the diner feels disconnected from the scenery. There is a sense of intimacy with the seascape and the way the light (and the birds, and the people) play on it—even in winter when it's solid ice.

## Recipes

# Top of the Park

After some years of seesawing back and forth between promise and payoff, this rooftop hideaway in the landmark Park Place Hotel has finally emerged as the first-class restaurant the hotel and the city deserve. The promise lies in an elegant combination of bandbox intimacy, big-city Art Deco sophistication, and a stunning view. The payoff is superb food.

The hotel dates to Depression days, and in the 1930s and the early postwar years it was the class act in Northern Michigan. Then came the motel era and visitors who wanted to drive right to their door and have a room on the beach. The Park Place slowly declined. Through the '80s the Top of the Park suffered through one faux pas after another as chefs and management teams came and went. Finally, the new owners, Traverse City's Rotary, hired one of their own to run the hotel. He brought in a new team—a veteran cruise-ship chef in Gerhard Ottinger, and Eduardo Marcenaro, a restaurant manager with extensive hotel experience. They've done all the right things, starting with a remodeling that enlarged the space and opened up the views while keeping the classic Art Deco look.

The menu is a similar mix of lovingly preserved tradition and an exciting new look. The traditionalists are happy the "Top" still has its long-time signature dish, steak Diane, and that it still sets out a big rib roast on weekends and regularly offers lamb chops with a rosemary demi-glace. A lot of diners these days, however, have become fans of the new ideas Ottinger brought with him. Many bear the stamp of southwestern influence, with cilantro, avocado, and various salsas making frequent appearances. One thing Ottinger regularly offers is a signature of his own (yes, we have the recipe for you), consisting of sautéed shiitake crab cakes on glass noodle and cucumber salad with a red pepper and cilantro vinaigrette. This was offered as an appetizer when we last saw it on a menu, but it ought to make a pretty nice main dish, too. What tempted us the last time we were there was pan-seared salmon served on a salsa of black bean, diced tomato, chopped avocado, onions and jalapeños, and sauced with creamed pan juices and saffron.

A stunning appetizer list greets grazers at the Top of the Park, as well. It includes such delights as a brandied morel-and-Portobello mushroom bisque, and tequila-marinated salmon Napoleons with avocado salsa and horseradish *crème fraîche*.

Part of the Rotarians' plan for the restaurant is to provide real-life training for advanced students in the local college's hospitality-industry school. Trust us, however, when we report there's nothing amateurish about this restaurant.

Everyone who (like us) thoroughly

## Top of the Park

Park Place Hotel
300 E. State St., Traverse City
616/946-5000

Dinners generally $15-20
Appetizers $4-6

enjoys going there, hopes the new beat goes on, because Traverse City is getting to be a right sophisticated, grown-up city, and it needs a classy, sophisticated, citified restaurant like the Top of the Park. And if you go on a weekend, head downstairs after dinner for a little schnapps with some of the blues and jazz for which the Park Place's Parlor is so famous Up North.

## Recipes

# Trillium

To many Northern Michigan loyalists, the entire Grand Traverse Resort seems out of place, jutting 17 stories above the cherry orchards. Moreover, the Trillium is on the top, which is a pretty citified place for a restaurant in a land of beach-stone fireplaces, knotty-pine dining rooms and whitewashed cottages.

This book, however, is about food, not architecture, and we find it odd that a lot of food-lovers—visitors and locals alike—seem to pass up the Trillium either because they object to the building or think of rooftop restaurants as unbearably snooty, ungodly expensive, or both. Frankly, we think the "Trill" is a comfy, reasonably-priced place with consistently good service and excellent food. The house signature dish of sautéed veal medallions on a cushion of spinach and Boursin and anointed with red-currant sauce, is enough to warrant a special trip regardless of location. And the location is spectacular. The view reaches from Traverse City to Old Mission, with an aerial perspective that provides lovely light

shows when fast-moving pools of sunshine wash the autumn landscape or swift lake-effect snow squalls whip across the bay under a cold, blue sky.

While the view won't change, we have to tread cautiously, because the resort's management plans to overhaul all the restaurants in 1997, from menu to decor to name. The Trillium's menu has already undergone surgery once in recent years, as they pared away some artistic, labor-intensive dishes and added a simpler, less-expensive tier of whitefish, steaks, chops and chicken. Plenty of adventure remains on the upper tier, however. We find nothing artless, for instance, about halibut baked in a blue-cheese crust, bathed in a tomato-cream sauce laced with salt bacon and garnished with scallops. Nothing very prosaic, either, about pan-seared venison with wild mushrooms and thyme sauce. Moreover, the Trillium is a grazer's paradise for its spectacular appetizers. Sautéed morel, shiitake and oyster mushrooms on vermicelli under a morel cream, paired with crab cakes

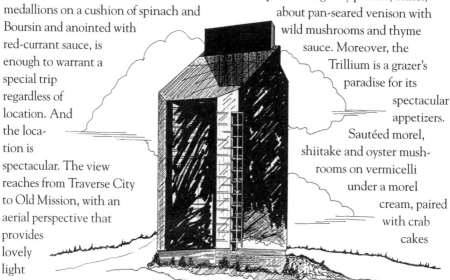

and fried leeks in roasted-pepper mayonnaise, is a dinner of appetizers fit for a king.

A well-drilled and knowledgeable staff helps you get the most out of the food and, with the backstage crew, gives the Trillium a major-league team that will remain no matter what else changes. To demonstrate how seriously the resort takes food and service, let us tell you about one night in 1995 when Chef Fritz Stieger and his crew prepared and served a five-course dinner to more than 600 fussy, top-dollar, business executives from a multinational Fortune 200 company. The trick was that they were spread out in six locations all over town, from a winery on Old Mission to the Opera House downtown and the Music House Museum in Acme. The entire meal, from hors d'oeuvres to dessert, was prepared in the resort's kitchens, then delivered and served at all six locations simultaneously. It was no chicken-à-la-king hotel banquet, either. After the hors d'oeuvre, came a salad of prosciutto-wrapped grilled shrimp on field greens with a basil vinaigrette; roasted beef tenderloin filet with sun-dried cherries, roasted walnuts, and a port-wine sauce; fettucine vegetables and dauphinoise potatoes.

---

## Trillium

Grand Traverse Resort
6800 US-31N, Traverse City
616/938-2100

Steakhouse dinners $15-17
    (incl. salad and vegetable)
Fancier entrees generally $20-23
Appetizers $6-8

---

Dessert? Oh, just 600 pears poached in Chablis, hollowed out and filled with hazelnut mousse and baked in phyllo, and set on individual plates on islands of almond marscapone in pools of cassis sauce. The meal got rave reviews from those worldly diners, whose company keeps returning to Grand Traverse Resort in part because the food and service are so good.

Finally, before we let you move on, we have to confess a certain conflict, perhaps even a bias, because one of us works for the resort. Proud of it, too. All we can add, now that we've told you this, is trust us: If you're a food-lover and have avoided the Trillium for reasons that don't have to do with food, you're missing a bet.

---

# Recipes

# Windows

L ast year, when a new little pâtisserie named Marifil's opened in Traverse City, it had a loyal clientele almost immediately, and the baguettes and eclairs, challah and cakes, cookies and truffles flew off the shelves. Since then, the proprietors have opened a second outlet Downtown and have begun producing ice cream, supplying desserts to restaurants, and offering deli salads, sandwiches and soups to the customers. To knowing locals, this success is no mystery. The coinage, "Marifil," combines the names of Marilyn and Phil Murray, whose restaurant, Windows, has long been famous for superb food, and especially for scandalously delicious desserts.

Anyone who would patronize Windows just for the sin of a few bonbons, however, would be making a grave error of omission. This is an excellent restaurant from end to end. It is not for dessert alone that readers of *Traverse* magazine regularly declare it their favorite in Northern Michigan. The Murrays provide polished and professional service, a world-class menu, and a sweeping view of Grand Traverse Bay from every table.

The menu always saves a place for familiar favorites, but generally offers something new and different as well. Phil lives and breathes food and is forever off on new adventures in the kitchen. Marilyn once confided that he sometimes even talks in his sleep about food.

Don't be surprised, if you've never enjoyed Windows, to find dishes of Creole lineage, for Phil's culinary career began in New Orleans. His signature dish remains a favorite called "Firecracker Pork." You'll find the complete recipe in this book, but we'll reveal here that it involves marinating pork tenderloin with garlic and vegetables in oil, cayenne pepper and minced ginger, then sautéing it all, simmering it in rich stock, and serving it atop bow-tie pasta garnished with cashews. We tell you this now only to demonstrate that Phil is not exactly tentative about flavors.

Another of his regular offerings is "Veal Winn Dixie," which is something of a moveable feast whose recipe he enjoys tinkering

with from time to time. The original came to him one day as he sat in a bar across from a Winn Dixie supermarket. One recent version called for veal sautéed in jalapeño butter with shrimp, crab and mushrooms. Nothing wishy-washy about that, either.

The fare at Windows is generous, and few patrons ever go away hungry. To arrive at his Cajun surf and turf, Phil adds a heap of barbecued shrimp to a generous cut of either grilled or blackened beef tenderloin. Even the vegetarian dishes you'll always find on the menu have a bit of heft and a downright positive attitude.

Light eaters need not despair, however. Windows puts a great deal into its appetizer list, too, so the menu is a grazer's delight. When we're in that frame of mind, we like to start with a cup of tomato-based turtle soup and follow with a dinner salad and a some barbecued shrimp or a gratin of morel, shiitake and Portobello mushrooms. Windows warmly

> ## Windows
> 7677 West Bay Shore Dr.
> Traverse City
> 616/941-0100
>
> Appetizers generally $4-9
> Entrees generally $16-25

welcomes grazers, and the staff seems to know without asking just what to bring to whom and when.

However you approach dinner at Windows, save room for one of those notorious desserts. Then enjoy one other delightful thing at Windows: the windows. Their wide-angle view of Grand Traverse Bay invites you to linger over an after-dinner drink while distant Traverse City turns into a necklace of lights as dusk falls across the water.

# Recipes

# Peninsula Wineries

It used to be that visitors came to Northern Michigan to swim, ski, fish, hike, or sail on the bay. Now they also come to see the farms and enjoy the output thereof. That's because some of the farms now grow grapes and the output thereof is wine. Surrounded by bays that temper extremes of temperature, Grand Traverse County's Old Mission Peninsula is as fine a place for vineyards as for orchards. Although the northern growing season is too short for decent reds, four peninsula wineries produce solid varietal whites, notably Riesling and Chardonnay. Moreover, the wineries are something of an attraction themselves. "Agritourism" is an official industry on the peninsula.

Foremost among them in this regard is Château Chantal, a handsome place surrounded by vineyards on the peninsula's highest hilltop. It not only has tasting and banquet rooms, it is a B&B as well, and it offers weekly "Jazz at Sunset" events when, for a small *prix fixe*, visitors enjoy a spread of bread, fruit and cheeses with their wines and watch the sun go down to a few hours of live music. The view of vineyards and bays is nothing short of spectacular, and the wines produced by proprietor Bob Begin and his vintner-partner Mark Johnson are among Michigan's best. *Château Chantal, 15900 Center Road, 616/223-4110.*

Oldest and best established of the wineries on Old Mission Peninsula is Château Grand Traverse, a mile or so south of Mapleton. In the 1980s Château Grand Traverse was first to demonstrate that Northern Michigan could produce good, varietal wines in commercial quantities. Their Chardonnay and Johannesburg Riesling are best sellers. The vineyards overlook both bays, and visitors are welcome daily for tasting and tours. The winery has banquet facilities as well. *Château Grand Traverse (616/223-0247)* is at 12239 Center Rd.

Relative newcomers to the Old Mission Peninsula winery roster are two small but proud vineyards established in the last few years. Bowers Harbor Vineyard is tucked into the sloping hillside between Mapleton on the hilltop and Bowers Harbor on the bay, and has a charming, rustic tasting-room that doubles as a banquet facility. *Bowers Harbor Vineyard (616/223-7615)* is at 2896 Bowers Harbor Rd., about a quarter mile east of Peninsula Drive. Farther out and on the peninsula's East Bay side is *Old Mission Winery (616/223-7276)*, the newest of the peninsula's operations, at 3175 Old Mission Rd.

# Other Seasons Other Reasons

This being the nearest thing Northern Michigan has to a big city, the whole range of restaurant styles is represented, and the discriminating food-lover is in no way limited to haute cuisine, or even to places where they know how to pronounce it. There are hole-in-the-wall delis and sandwich shoppes where even the most hurried workday luncher can find bright and healthful salads, savory homemade soups and freshly baked bread. You'll find cozy bistros and coffee houses with a continental flavor, as well as neighborhood saloons whose hardwood floors still bear the scars of loggers' boots.

After a long day's work, Traverse Citians find it's a cinch to bag the KP on the spur of the moment and go out for a truly good dinner in convivial surroundings without getting all gussied up or spending an arm and a leg. And at lunch time, folks who work or shop in TC know they don't have to choose between brown-bagged tuna or 2000 deep-fried calories

dispensed through a drive-up window.

There are few seasonal restaurants here, for Traverse City is a thoroughly year-round place nowadays. This is not to say things don't slow down in winter, because they do. But any restaurant good enough to satisfy the serious food-lover will have enough business to stay open all year. Some of us think the slower seasons are the nicest, because there are seldom any waiting lines, and we can linger over an extra cup of coffee and not worry about keeping someone else waiting.

## Sleder's

Lord knows how many millhands, sailors, and Prohibition dandies have bellied up to the bar since Louis Sleder built his saloon in 1887. For sure, Sleder's is one of Michigan's oldest taverns, although it is now a relatively tame neighborhood place. It is no less a landmark, however. The present owners, Brian and Deb Cairns, have worked hard to preserve it all, from the classic,

## Sail Ho!

If the mystery of the Big Lake is one of the things that draws you Up North, why not really connect with it aboard one of the stately, picturesque tall ships that regularly sail Lake Michigan and Grand Traverse Bay on cruises ranging from two hours to six days. The stately, graceful schooner *Manitou* offers cruises of three, five and six days. Three-day cruises simply go where wind and weather take them—the Manitous, perhaps, or around Leelanau. On several five-day "island-hopper" cruises she explores legendary Beaver Island and the mysterious archipelago surrounding it. Twice a summer she sails from Detour Village in the Upper Peninsula on six-day voyages through the fabled North Channel of Lake Huron. Fares start at $325 for three days. The schooner *Malabar* makes two-hour day cruises on West Grand Traverse Bay from her berth in Traverse City. In May (when she's a floating classroom for local schools during the week) public cruises are offered only on weekends. She cruises daily in July and August, and six days a week in June and September. Following the evening cruises, she becomes a floating B&B whose guests share breakfast the next morning with the crew. This is a rare treat, because the *Malabar* always seems to have a fabulous cook. For schedules and fares: *Traverse Tall Ship Co., 13390 S. West Bay Shore Dr., Traverse City, 616/941-2000.*

including a moose that first-timers are dared to kiss. The hearty fare includes monumental sandwiches and half-pound burgers, either beef or buffalo from the herd south of town. There is rich bean soup laced with ham; there are creamy slaw and some of the finest fries and onion rings in captivity. If you're uneasy in what is essentially still a bar, there's an adjacent dining room with full dinners after five, from char-grilled chicken and steak, ribs, perch, trout and whitefish, to a smattering of Tex-Mex. You can satisfy a powerful hunger here for less than $10, and Friday evenings mean all the fish you can handle for considerably less. Smelt, too. *Sleder's, 717 Randolph St., Traverse City. 616/947-9213.*

stamped-tin ceiling right down to the polished brass rail under the massive mahogany bar. Sleder's is favored by workday lunchers and the TGIF crowd, and by busy families who gather around time-worn tables among the yellowing mementoes of Traverse City's past, including a glorious old Wurlitzer jukebox by the door. Looking on are whole walls full of stuffed animals,

## Bowery

Tucked in the back rooms behind the stately Bowers Harbor Inn (of which it is a more gently priced adjunct), this is one of Northern Michigan's most popular restaurants. That's as true in January as in July, perhaps because so many among its loyal clientele are year-round Peninsula neighbors who think the Bowery serves up the best barbecued ribs in Northern Michigan. The decor is all beams and mullioned glass and barn siding, and the dining is far more laid back and casual than in the inn's white-tableclothed precincts out front. If ribs aren't your thing, try a mess of perch. They, too, are a treat. While drinks are generous, the selection of beers is prodigious. *The Bowery, 13512 Peninsula Dr., Traverse City. 616/223-4222.*

# Mode's

Bob and Anita Mode's Bum Steer in downtown Traverse City is a perennial favorite among beef lovers, and it's a cinch to find even if you've never been there. Just follow your nose to the source of the awesome aroma of steaks on the grill. That's the only advertising Bob Mode does—or needs. Bob himself presides over the grill in his minuscule kitchen, turning out world-class steaks, prime rib, surf-and-turf, lamb and ribs. All come in the company of salad from a bar and dependably big, fresh bakers wrapped in foil. The classic steakhouse fare might be a bit dated in the '90s, but for nostalgics who crave it, it's the best. This smoker-friendly establishment is a haven for diehards, but the A/C system is so awesome that plenty of persnickety nonsmokers are drawn there for the thick, rare, grilled beef

and the convivial, club-like ambience. The service is fast and practiced, and the prices are as easygoing as the atmosphere. *Mode's Bum Steer, 125 State St., Traverse City. 616/947-9832.*

# Boathouse

Opened in 1995, this is the latest in a line of restaurants operated in Traverse City by one Batsakis or another since the 1930s. The proprietor here is John Batsakis, who used to own the U&I Lounge downtown. The lineage traces to Pete Batsakis's Pete's Cafe on Front Street, back when the hits on the jukebox were by the Andrews Sisters. The Boathouse is in a former general store-deli on the beach at Bowers Harbor, thoroughly remodeled into one of Northern Michigan's cheeriest, airiest places. There is a cozy bar up front with a cushioned window seat, and in the bright dining room, picture windows provide the glories of sunsets over the bay. The fare is straightforward steaks and seafood and interesting pastas, and a highlight of any meal is the basket of hot popovers with honey-butter. Thanks to all that family restaurant experience, Batsakis's staff had its act together from day one. *The Boathouse, 14039 Peninsula Dr., Traverse City. 616/223-4030.*

# Bon Appétit

It took a while for foodies to tumble to this delightful cafe after it opened in 1995, even though it's in a conspicuously bright yellow house flying le Tricolore smack-dab on Front Street just a few blocks from the heart of town. Maybe this is because it is such a radical departure from the decidedly American establishment that preceded it. Bon Appétit is proudly French, and we suggest you not challenge its authenticity lest the proprietaire exclaim taisez-vous! That would be Anne Pujos, who came to Traverse City with her husband to design high-tech archery equipment. The archery deal soured, but they loved living Up Nord, so while he set up his own arrow-distributing company, they opened a restaurant, too. Never mind that she did not have beaucoup de restaurant experience. Food just comes naturally to a woman from Lyon, and running a business comes naturally, too, because that woman from Lyon used to be a cosmetics marketing executive. Bon Appétit is a marketers' delight: simply furnished but bright and cheery on even the dreariest days, and serving up delightful quiches and pot pies, savory soups, delicious salads that brighten and cheer the lunch-hour no end. The Sunday breakfasts here are more or less Américain, although augmented by crêpes, croissants, omelettes and (naturellement) French toast. By evening, the menu really dresses up, when chef Paul Hughes whips up grilled salmon, char-broiled beef, smoked chicken pasta and (on Fridays) a

## Away From the Crowd II

We're going to cheat a bit here, and suggest a picnic that isn't really in Traverse City. But there's no way to get there without going through the city, because our secluded spot is on Old Mission Peninsula—16 miles out, at the very tip. Before leaving civilization, pick up a baguette at Marifil's bakery on 14th Street, and maybe a truffle or some cookies for dessert. You'll need fruit, of course, and just up Division Street you'll find the Meijer store. Not exactly a romantic little fruit stand, maybe, but trust us. No matter how exotic the fruit or veg you're after, if someone grows it they probably have it. (Of course, the Farmer's Market downtown is a must, but it's open only on Wednesday and Saturday mornings in season.) Next, head down to Folgarelli's on Front Street and have them wrap up a chunk of your favorite cheese before you head up Center Road (that's M-37, stranger). About 13 miles out, watch for vineyards, and stop in at one of the wineries and fetch a nice, cold bottle of Riesling or Chardonnay. Back on Center Road, park by the stone monument at the very end, walk past the lighthouse to the shore, and there you are. The whole tip of the peninsula is a park and it's yours—beach, rocks, woods and all, including a lot of nice, shallow water for wading. If it's winter, there's even a cross-country ski loop.

knockout seafood paella. The only thing we'd advise against is duck, a consistent disappointment. The proprietress herself does the tartes, quiches, and desserts. For the moment, alas, *il n'y a pas de* wine list. Later, perhaps . . . *Bon Appétit, 810 E. Front St., Traverse City. 616/947-2634.*

## Left Bank Café

The casual visitor to Traverse City might easily overlook this compact cafe on the banks of the Boardman a few blocks east of the heart of town. Food-loving locals know it well, however, as the source of healthful salads, interesting sandwiches, potent homemade soups and luscious sweets. Find it once and you'll remember the way back. The tireless owner-chef, Jackie Honea, is a word person, so she isn't kidding when she advertises that the cafe also does "spectacular catering." You'll find her recipe for their sun-dried-tomato and basil roulades in the back of our book, along with the secret to the Left Bank's smoked turkey and wild rice muffins. Mmm! Much of the lunch trade here is carry-out, but there are about a dozen seats at tables close enough together to improve the odds of

conversation that's as interesting as the food. *The Left Bank Café, 439 E. Front St., Traverse City. 616/929-9060.*

## Omelette Shoppes

Take the advice of any Traverse City food-lover about where you might get a good breakfast, and you'll probably find yourself at one of Dick Dell'Acqua's two Omelette Shoppes. The unanimity of the clientele is nothing short of amazing, and for good reasons: The Omelette Shoppes will serve you the kind of solid, old-fashioned American breakfast that most other restaurants only dream of. They'll have the freshest of fruit, the hottest of breakfast coffee, and the lightest, fluffiest pancakes and French toast. The syrup will be maple, the bacon crisp, the sausage snappily flavorful. You'll get perfectly golden toast, rich rolls, buttery croissants and moist-hot muffins, and your eggs or omelettes, however you want them, will be done with a precision to make a hen proud. Yes, there might be a waiting line at busy periods (no wonder!), but don't let that deter you because the wait is seldom long. Dell'Acqua's staff, as efficient as it is attentive and friendly, has mastered the art of moving people in and out without hurrying a soul. If the Omelette Shoppes have a flaw, it is excess choice and a staff so well drilled that they recite the choices faster than your mind can react before breakfast. Even at lunch, it's a bit daunting to order a sandwich and then try to decipher "D'y'waniton-raisinoatbrancherrype-caneight-grain-wholewheatorsourdough?" Oh, yeah: All those baked goods are made on the premises, and (more good news) they are available to go, too. *Omelette Shoppes, 1209 E. Front St., Traverse City, 616/946-0590, and 124 Cass St., Traverse City, 616/946-0912.*

## Panda North

The only oriental restaurant in Northern Michigan to which we return enthusiastically, this friendly little place is tucked away in the Logan's Landing shopping center where Traverse City's South Airport Road crosses the Boardman River. What sets it apart is less the menu than the execution and service. The food is your basic American-style Chinese, from crab Rangoon, egg-drop soup and egg rolls to moo goo gai pan, moo shu pork and fortune cookies. All is invariably well prepared from good ingredients, and what's supposed to be crisp is crisp, what's not is not. There's seldom a wait, orders are taken and

## Edible Events

Traverse City, of course, is home to the granddaddy of all Up North food events, the National Cherry Festival—10 days each July full of rides, games, parades, and pie-eating contests. It dates to the "Blessing of the Blossoms" in the 1920s, and draws hundreds of thousands of visitors. Other annual events may draw fewer visitors but are of no less interest to the food-lover. The Traverse Symphony combines music and food each winter with post-concert benefit dinners in February and March at premier restaurants. Each May, locals flock to the campus of Northwestern Michigan College for the NMC Barbecue, a happy, fund-raising pig-out for the school. Early each autumn, the tireless volunteers of the local March of Dimes lure top-drawer restaurant chefs from miles around to their fund-raising Chef's Dinner cook-off and auction at the Park Place Hotel. Around Valentine's Day sweet-toothed chocoholics help support the City Opera House at a Chocolate Extravangaza there. And in June, there's an art fair at the Old Mission Tavern, where you can enjoy some of the artist-owner's blue-cheese-spinach-bacon pasta with your *objets trouvé* metalworks and impressionist landscapes.

delivered promptly, and the teapot is refilled before it gets cold. Reasonable prices make it a nice lunchtime getaway or an impromptu evening out. *Panda North, 2038 S. Airport Rd., Traverse City. 616/929-9722.*

## Resources

If you want to find a whole bunch of food-lovers in one place at one time, go to the open-air market on the banks of the Boardman River every Wednesday and

Saturday from early June to mid-October. In a land of roadside fruit stands and farm markets, it's the biggest and best. Growers come from all corners of the state to peddle their fresh, seasonal fruits, berries, vegetables, herbs, and flowers from folding tables and stands and the backs of trucks. Here you can find asparagus and strawberries in spring, blueberries and cherries in summer, the crisp new lettuces, plump broccoli and succulent beans in summer, and the ripest apples, squashes and pumpkins in autumn. It's first-come, first-served for stall space, so you never know who'll be selling what, where, and food-lovers know to arrive early to be sure of getting the ripest, freshest and plumpest before things get picked over. The market opens at 8 and closes at midday (earlier if the stalls sell out). If you need fresh produce you can't find at the market, you'll probably find it at Traverse City's Meijer store on Division Street. Hundreds of serious cooks in search of exotic produce put up with the discount-shopping throngs because Meijer is known for its amazing variety. There's one more must stop for the food-loving cook in Traverse City, and that's the stretch of Front Street between Wadsworth and Division. It's a sort of Gourmet's Alley. There you'll find Folgarelli's Market and Deli and Mary's Kitchen Port, Burritt's Meat Market and Carlson's Fishery and Potter's Bakery, all within a short stroll. Folgarelli's is a classic delicatessen with an Italian accent and a food-to-go counter. It specializes in hard-to-find ethnic foods both tinned and fresh, and has wines and freshly baked breads as well. Mary's is a combination kitchenware store and deli, with delicious luncheon salads and sinfully rich desserts prepared on the premises by Mary Boudjalis and her son, Mike. Burritt's is where you'll find such things as the perfect veal for scallopini, and at Carlson's right next door, they will not only sell you the town's freshest seafood and Great Lakes

## Never a Dull Moment

Cross-country skiing is king in winter, and each January TC is host to the Grand Travers races, which serve as a sort of warm-up for February's North American Vasa, the continent's second-largest cross-country ski competition. April brings the Piano Festival competition to Interlochen Arts Academy, and then life moves outdoors. One Saturday each June, magnificent schooners from Great Lakes ports convene on Grand Traverse Bay for a "Tall Ships Rendezvous" (It was a "race" until two of the stately vessels collided a few years ago). In July there are the annual outdoor art fair at Northwestern Michigan College and the antique-and-collectibles show at Traverse City's Civic Center. It's back indoors in November, for Dennos Museum Center's Festival of Trees and the 100,000 bulbs of Grand Traverse Resort's Northwoods Festival of Lights. Then in December, who can resist visiting the City Opera House for the Festival of Trains?

fish, they will ask if you want the filets pin-boned. The sweet-toothed crowd adores Marifil's, the pâtisserie-bakery owned by the proprietors of Windows Restaurant and featuring pastries it's famous for, as well as cookies, breads, ice creams and other dessert-time treats. There are two Marifils, on 14th Street and Front Street. Finally, for wine in the Traverse City area, there's no better than Bob and Mary Ann Paulinski's Village Wine Shop at Front and Peninsula. They're knowledgeable, helpful, and stock a wide and interesting variety. It's the North's best wine shop.

## All About Whitefish

Rare is the successful restaurant in Northern Michigan that serves no whitefish. This mild, white-fleshed freshwater creature of 2-6 pounds is more than a local favorite. It's a staple, and has been since long before any Europeans came visiting. There is nothing new about food-lovers' affinity for whitefish.

In ancient days, Ojibwas in canoes netted them in the Great Lakes and scooped them from the rapids at Sault Ste. Marie. The fish they called *ticaming* is still the mainstay of Native American commercial netters. Rod-and-reel anglers catch whitefish by trolling with downriggers or jigging in deep water on still days.

Those Indians, the earliest locals, caught them by the hundreds and preserved them with smoke for winter subsistence. The tourists caught right on. In 1703 a French explorer, the Baron La Hontan, reported on a "white fish" so good that "all sorts of sauces spoil it." The French historian deCharlevoix, traveling the Great Lakes in 1721, wrote that "whether fresh or salted, nothing of the fish kind can excel it." A century later, the Indian agent Henry Rowe Schoolcraft wrote in his journal that of all the fish in the Great Lakes, "the white fish is most esteemed for the richness and delicacy of its flavour." (*Chacun à son goût*, as the French say, because Schoolcraft added, "We can not, however, agree with the Baron La Hontan.")

The traditional way of preparing whitefish Up North is "planked," that is, roasted on a slab of wood, usually oak or cedar. This is how Indians did it before Europeans introduced the sauté pan to the New World. Modern chefs still serve it that way, as well as boiled, broiled, fried, baked, grilled, and sautéed. As *The Outing* magazine said in 1905, however whitefish is cooked, "one taste, and you are an enthusiastic admirer for life."

## Recipes

# Charlevoix— Torch—Elk—Boyne

This marvelous stretch of Michigan's west coast is a hilly, lake-studded delight for all who love being outdoors. It is a place for anglers and sailors, golfers and skiers, hikers and snowmobilers. The coastline is marked on the south by the charming little harbor town of Elk Rapids and on the north by the busy port of Charlevoix. Inland are forested, orchard-covered hills overlooking dozens of lakes.

Among them are Lake Charlevoix and the famous Chain of Lakes, with nearly 100 miles of water meandering from Elk Rapids to Bellaire and beyond. The largest of the chain—Torch and Elk lakes—are long and deep, with the same clear blue-green water as Lake Michigan. Linking them are several lesser lakes, connected by gently flowing streams and marshes teeming with wildlife. In the weedy shallows and dark-blue depths lurk lunker trout, bass, pike and muskie. Along one of the connecting streams, the boardwalks of the Grass River Natural Area give nature-lovers a close-up view of waterfowl in their natural habitat. There's nothing unusual about scouting out a bald eagle in these parts. And Antrim County is famous Up North for its wild turkeys. Whole flocks of them are likely to stroll out of the roadside woods in front of your car and make you wonder why on earth turkey hunters think them so smart.

Lodging abounds on the main coastal artery, US-31, and charming B&Bs await in Elk Rapids, Bellaire, Alden, Charlevoix and Ellsworth, within walking distance of some of the North's best restaurants.

The area's largest community, Charlevoix, is a shopper's haven, with art galleries, antique shops and boutiques with everything from high fashion to the funkiest resort wear. The city surrounds a deep-water harbor. One way lies Lake Michigan and the world, and in the other direction Lake Charlevoix stretches inland to lively, rejuvenated Boyne City and East Jordan and its scenic Jordan River, much favored by canoeists.

At Elk Rapids down the coast is one of the finest marinas on the Great Lakes, within a three-minute stroll of a classic home-town main street with a grocery, drugstore, hardware, laundry, bakery, post office, and movie theater. Among them are galleries and shops you can browse for art, antiques and collectibles to dress up the cottage. The mayor himself runs the movie theater, built in 1940, and will proudly tell you it boasts the world's largest (and, possibly, only) black-light ceiling mural.

There's a ton to do in this part of Michigan, but save time for dinner, because the area also has more good restaurants per capita than any other.

# Grey Gables

When Darren and Kelly Romano took over the kitchen as chefs and co-proprietors of Charlevoix's venerable Grey Gables Inn, they made important changes without reshaping the charming old package. They left the Victorian-parlor decor in the dining rooms, but updated the menu no end. It would be easy for the passing tourist to overlook this unobtrusive little place on Belvedere Street, but food-loving locals know it well enough to keep things busy even on snowy winter nights.

The Romanos are a team. She's up early doing the pastries and breads, and after he arrives in mid-morning to get dinner underway, she takes time out for their infant. She's back by evening to tend to business out front with their third co-proprietor, her dad, Gary Anderson.

Darren's menu is solid fare, anchored by such classics as barbecued pork ribs, rack of lamb, stuffed pork chop and prime rib. "It might be a little rich," Darren admits, "but I believe in giving value."

Frankly, we think the real value at Grey Gables is up front on the menu. Darren's appetizers are a grazer's treasure trove, and it's a cinch to make a grand meal without venturing into entree territory. Here's a sample: Start with a bowl of mushroom bisque or sherried five-onion soup. Follow with a classic Greek or Caesar salad, and then round things out with an order of escargots wrapped in phyllo. That little three-course stroll among the appetizers would satisfy any but the most dedicated trencherman—for about the price of a typical dinner without soup or appetizer.

Grey Gables is not for the light eater, but there are concessions. Cross Fisheries is right across the street, and whitefish, perch and walleye are generally on offer— broiled, poached or sautéed with lemon-caper sauce. The cholesterol-shy will appreciate Darren's vegetable plate with roasted redskins, and his veggie pasta Provençal.

But his forte is clearly the meaty entrees whose very names evoke images of NFL linemen: beef Wellington, rack of lamb, stuffed pork chop, prime rib, sirloin, and whiskey-marinated chicken. Just between us, however, don't let too many visits pass without trying those escargots. Darren sautés them with tomato in ample garlic-chive butter, then wraps it all up with roasted pine nuts in a delicate phyllo envelope for baking.

The other star of any meal at Grey Gables shows up right at the opening curtain, in the form of a basket of Kelly's sweet, little crescent scones and lovely French bread. And even at the risk of overdosing on carbs, spud-lovers should save room for Darren's whipped potatoes. They may be the best you'll find north of the 45th parallel, and if they don't come with whatever you order, you can always

have them à la carte.

Grey Gables is not fancy, showy, or right out there amongst the tourists. But it's worth the excursion a block or so off the main drag, especially on weekends, when you're likely to find a lively blues combo in the lounge.

---

## Grey Gables

308 Belvedere Street
Charlevoix
616/547-9261

Entrees typically $15-17
à la carte appetizers $5-7
Special salads $5-6

---

# Monte Bianco

Few restaurants can be defined as much by a moment as by cuisine, but John and Mary Kelly's Monte Bianco in Boyne City is one of them. They opened the restaurant in 1993, and the moment came soon after, when the chef left one day in mid-July, at the very height of the season. The Kellys are managers, not cooks, but they could have tried to fake it for the sake of cash flow until they found a new chef. They know the value of a good reputation, however, and they treasure theirs. So they closed the doors for three days, smack in mid-season, rather than compromise the product.

That says much about Monte Bianco, and explains its loyal clientele. Even though it is somewhat off the beaten track, still rather new, and not widely known, we consider it a hidden gem. It is certainly the finest Italian restaurant in Northern Michigan.

It is not typical, however, either in menu or ambience. Tomato makes only cameo appearances, and such staples as garlic and olive, prosciutto and basil, Gorgonzola and mozzarella play mere supporting roles. The food at Monte Bianco depends more on fine, fresh ingredients, imaginative combinations, and meticulous preparation. The Kellys call it "San Francisco Italian," but that's too simple a description for the delights they'll set before you.

They've made a sort of signature dish of walleye in a surprisingly fluffy mozzarella crust, which comes costumed in a different sauce every night. One night it will be pesto, the next a flavorful relish of crushed ripe olives, tomatoes and garlic.

The Kellys used to own a restaurant in San Francisco, but came to love Northern Michigan on visits to Mary's brother. They arrived permanently in 1992 and bought a run-down old roadhouse outside Boyne City called the Nordic Bar. They spent a year gutting it and

installing a fresh, new, look—sort of cool, relaxed, understated contemporary-Deco. Their chef, a friend from San Francisco, was a Thai who had worked in Italian restaurants. It was an improbable combination that worked, and Monte Bianco clicked in its very first season. There's just no denying good food, efficient service, and happy atmosphere.

Now, under chef Glenn Gerring, the menu is essentially the same and the kitchen does no less justice to *pollo piccata* and *scampi e capellini*. The *vitello* Monte Bianco is still the same elegantly simple affair of veal medallions sautéed in butter with lemon, mushrooms and parsley.

The classic Italian menu begins with *antipasti* including carpaccio with oil, black pepper and mustard sauce, and a pizzetta with garlic and cambozola. There is minestrone, of course, and salads of the freshest, crispest greens even in January.

And naturally there are pasta dishes—penne, for instance, with chicken, black olives and tomatoes tossed with oil and garlic, or *linguine frutti di mare* in which prawns, scallops, mussels and roasted

---

## Monte Bianco

02911 Boyne City Rd.
Boyne City
616/582-3341

Appetizers $7-8
Pasta dinners $10-13
Other dinners $12-19
Desserts $4-5

---

garlic swim in a tomato sauce. We are particularly fond of Monte Bianco's homemade shrimp raviolis, astonishingly light even under a basil cream and vodka sauce.

On top of all this, Monte Bianco is a happy place to be. Mary is all calm efficiency in the dining room and John presides at the bar. You'll find no silent couples staring at the walls. The tides of animated conversation ebb and flow in the softly lighted dining room, swirling about lively groups of skiers, cottagers and locals laughing and talking and having a good time over excellent food.

---

## Recipes

# On the Edge

Begun a few years ago as Pete and Mickey's by the folks who brought us Tapawingo, this place became On the Edge in 1995 when it was bought by its young chef, John Norman, and maitre d', Carla Bradley. Happy to say, not much has changed but the name. The colorful, happy-go-lucky spot on Charlevoix's Bridge Street, right by the drawbridge, is no less fun for new ownership, and Norman hasn't stopped producing the sorts of delightful surprises the place is known for among its regulars. Better, it is now an all-day, every-day, year-round restaurant that no longer closes for five months when the last leaf-watcher goes south.

On the Edge is aptly named. Not only is it the house restaurant for the Edgewater Inn, its youthful chef is a risk-taking adventurer in the kitchen. You never know what new treat he'll surprise you with. Grilled shrimp teriyaki today, and tomorrow maybe whitefish baked in an almond crust with a roasted red-pepper sauce. And since On the Edge is open all day, you can have your smoked whitefish cakes with horseradish cream, eggs and potatoes for breakfast, then again for lunch or dinner with corn relish or salsa.

He calls his food "modern American," but we are inordinately fond of Norman's Mediterranean-style shrimp fettucine. He throws sautéed shrimp into the pasta with a light, white-wine sauce, punctuates it with pine nuts, excites it with garlic, brightens it up with sun-dried tomatoes, and finally softens the edges with grated Parmesan. Washed down with a glass of Joliesse Chardonnay, the house white, it's a perfect finish to a long sail up the coast or an afternoon's browsing the shops and galleries of Bridge Street.

The atmosphere is decidedly casual, although in an urbane resort town like Charlevoix you'll find some pretty dressy casual in high season and might feel a bit out of place in truly grubbies. There are beautiful people to be seen here as well as faithful locals. Part of the fun of On the Edge is the decor and scenery.

The ambience is sort of primary-color, geometric, high-tech funky. If conversation flags, the view of the harbor and drawbridge from the newly enclosed sun porch is interesting. Truly dedicated sedentarians can work up an appetite watching the boats come and go and the drawbridge go up and down.

Norman is one of those naturals, an accomplished chef without formal training from whose imagination interesting dishes seem to spring spontaneously. Maybe it has something to do with being the town mayor's son; more likely it's just native talent enhanced by association with those Tapawingo people. The restaurant's success also has much to do with Bradley, whose brother owns

three restaurants at the other end of Bridge Street. Whatever it is, adventuresome diners in search of interesting food will always find something to talk about On the Edge.

---

## On The Edge

100 S. Michigan
Charlevoix
616/547-2929

Appetizers $4-7
Salads $2-8
Entrees generally $10-15
Desserts about $4

---

# Recipes

# One Water Street

This may be the most ambitious restaurant in Northern Michigan. Its all-encompassing menu has nine entrees on a page of "favorites," 11 more on a "Michigan Heartland" page, another page with four dinners "from the grill," four steak dinners, and three surf-and-turf combination platters. That's after a page of 10 appetizers, of which one (modestly called a "sampler") incorporates oysters Rockefeller, chilled shrimp, chicken wings in barbecue sauce, smoked whitefish, seafood sausage, vegetables, dip and crackers. Add four soups and six salads to the menu, and you inevitably conclude that this restaurant seeks to be all things to all people.

It certainly is popular, drawing crowds of Lake Charlevoix cottagers in summer and Boyne Mountain skiers in winter. One attraction is the consistently pleasant, efficient service common to Stafford's Hospitality restaurants, of which it is one.

One Water Street, a sort of 1980s interpretation of 1890s design, was built a decade ago on the site of old docks in Boyne City. The decor covers as much ground as the menu: The foyer is simulated Victorian, one dining room is Gay Nineties, another is beams and timbers, the cocktail lounge is hunting-lodge taxidermy, and in summer there's dining on a deck by the lake.

The heart of the menu is the page labeled "Michigan Heartland," consisting largely of entrees built around such indigenous foods as whitefish, trout, perch, duck, pheasant and morels. Whitefish are offered three ways, including planked with broiled tomato and the usual surrounding of duchesse potatoes. The rainbow trout is stuffed with spinach, bacon, mushroom, leeks, capers and herbs, dusted with crushed walnut, and sautéed, and the perch come as they do at all Stafford's restaurants— sautéed in butter with garlic and sherry.

The appetizers, all nicely prepared, range from basic shrimp cocktail, escargots and bluepoints, to a grilled sausage of walleye, shrimp and scallops served

with herbed mayonnaise.

For the most part, the fare is conservative, for there is not much time for experiment in a kitchen with so much variety to contend with. But the standards are high and you can count on the service, even on busy nights when the crowd overflows into the lounge.

On those nights when you get together with the whole gang to go out to dinner, but have trouble agreeing on the kind of place you want to go, One Water Street is a good bet. There's enough choice there to keep a lot of tastes happy.

## One Water Street

1 Water St.
Boyne City
616/582-3434

Appetizers generally $6-7
Heartland Menu dinners $16-25
Other dinners $16-30
   (Dinners incl. soup or salad)
Extensive specialty beers $3-5

## Recipes

# The Rowe

For the true food-lover, dinner at The Rowe is a pilgrimage, because this is more than just a fine restaurant. It is also a shrine of sorts. This is where regional cooking in the provincial, French fashion arrived in Northern Michigan, at the hands of a one-time history teacher named Wes Westhoven.

That was in 1972, when Westhoven wearied of teaching and came north (like so many urban escapees) to live in vacationland and pursue his interests—in this case, food. He had grown up in his folks' restaurant near Toledo and studied the business in college, and now he bought a little knotty-pine, plate-lunch roadhouse called The Rowe Inn. There, in an era when steaks-chops-chicken was about as haute as the cuisine got in Northern Michigan, Westhoven introduced the area to the European notion of "regional" cooking. He did fresh, local asparagus in June, local strawberries in July and raspberries in August. He served local perch and whitefish without (gasp!) benefit of

deep frying, and seasoned them with inventive sauces and locally grown herbs.

Some locals were a bit puzzled at first, Westhoven recalls, especially when he headed for the woods in spring to pick morels. "Maybe they thought morels were poisonous," he says, "or that we were too poor to buy food from the grocery like everyone else." Today, some of those same people show up each spring to sell him morels they've picked. Inspired by Westhoven's frequent visits in France, the fare at The Rowe has a decidedly Provençal accent these days, but it is still Northern Michigan food.

Westhoven has given the region chefs as well as food; Tapawingo's Pete Peterson and Jim Milliman of Hattie's both were once chefs at The Rowe—a mantle worn quite gracefully in recent years by an Ellsworth native, Kathy Ruis.

Although his best-selling menu item is a white chocolate brownie, Westhoven prefers to think of pecan-stuffed morels as the house specialty. "It's a very special dish that I've never seen done as well as we do it," he says, with the

credibility of a champ.

Don't ask him, however, what kind of a restaurant he runs. "I hate that question," he'll answer. "We cook what we like. The idea is to emphasize Northern Michigan stuff. Cherries, morels, fish. We work with French techniques, but that doesn't make us a French restaurant. It just makes us a good restaurant."

Rowe regulars tend to understand that a good restaurant need not be fancy, formal or elegant, but that good meals require good wine and lively conversation. Much of the charm of The Rowe is in a total experience that transcends mere menu. The Rowe is still a knotty-pine roadhouse, whose proprietor, on a slow night, may well pull up a chair for a little conversation. When he does, the subject is certain to turn to wine. The Rowe has an extraordinary cellar, and Wes may sit down with a bottle or two and a couple of extra glasses, so you can sniff and swirl and sip while you talk of food, wine, love, war, music, art and politics. "Wine," he says, "is as important as the food, and together they make something far more than the two separate entities."

Among The Rowe's special events are off-season Sunday wine brunches, where a modest *prix fixe* brings a starter of eggs

## The Rowe

East Jordan Rd.
Ellsworth
616/588-7351

Appetizers $6-8
Dinners generally $22-28
   (include soup, salad)
Wines $20-200
Also wine at retail from one of the
   Midwest's top cellars.

Benedict, a sumptuous buffet that usually includes a classic *boeuf bourguignon*, and an array of wines for sampling. The Rowe also does a dazzling Madrigal Christmas Dinner each December, "Morel Festival" feasts two Sundays each May, and pricey but spectacular "Great Wines" dinners in April and November.

Perhaps the most special event at The Rowe is one that occurs almost nightly, in the form of a waitress named Annie Hines. She is a fixture, and if you're prudish or prone to blushing, ask for another server. Whenever Annie senses a lull at your table, she is likely to pause at your elbow and drop a hilariously bawdy joke, like a *bouquet garni*, into the broth of your conversation.

## Recipes

# Spencer Creek

Whenever anyone asks our opinion of this charming little restaurant on the eastern shore of lovely Torch Lake, we have a ready answer: We like it so much we chose to have our wedding dinner there after being married on the lawn by the lake. The proprietors in those days were Jeff and Laura Kohl, who have since sold the restaurant, but we are happy to say that under the new owners—Kathy, Bill and Mike Peterson—Spencer Creek is as good as ever, if not even better. It is one of the top half dozen restaurants in Michigan. We return every April on our wedding anniversary, and as often as we can at other times of year.

Spencer Creek is in a simple, two-story, frame, Edwardian house in the center of tiny Alden, with an expanse of tree-shaded lawn that slopes down to the shore of Torch Lake. Inside, in the three quiet, intimate dining rooms, all is oak woodwork and white table-cloth and the muted glint of soft light on polished crystal. Outside beyond the windows, sunsets fling their crimson and gold across the lake.

Into this quiet, charming setting, from Mike Peterson's kitchen come marvelously conceived and executed meals. They begin with the little complimentary, savory "treat" that everyone receives simply to stimulate the senses. It is a delightful custom, known in England as a "starter," which the Kohls introduced and the Petersons carry on.

Then come intriguing appetizers and soups, rich with the flavors of the season. In spring, look for fresh mint or tender asparagus; in summer, chilled cantaloupe, perhaps, garnished with plum. The simple flavors weave complex melodies, and all is presented with a sculptor's artistry.

Salads follow, no less interesting. Pears and Gorgonzola on airy Bibb with just enough vinaigrette to tease. Baby spinach with phyllo croutons that have been spread with crushed pecan and cambozola and dressed with an artful mixture of vinegar, lime juice, honey, sour cherries and oil. (The appetizers and salads are such delights that Spencer Creek is a grazer's heaven when it is offering its slightly less pricey "light dinners" of a salad and two appetizers.)

The entrees rest on simple foundations—salmon, trout, lamb, beef, duck—then spire upwards to support exquisite finishing touches of garnish and sauce. Rainbow trout is encrusted with cashew and served with spinach, corn bread and a lemon-chive sauce; grilled pork is served with an onion and tomato compote and a peppery barbecue sauce.

Mike Peterson, the chef among the trio-in-charge, arrived in Alden after training at the Culinary Institute of America and a stint at the Westin in Hilton Head, S.C. He regards his efforts at Spencer Creek as French, and seems to have resisted the fashionable "fusion" of recent years. You're not likely to find much salsa or Thai fish sauce here. What you will find in his recipes are scallops and lemon, shallots and dry wines, cream and butter, wild rice and hazelnut, morels when available, and fresh vegetables and herbs bought from neighboring purveyors or grown outside the door.

## Spencer Creek

5166 Helena St.
Alden
616/331-6147

Appetizers $5-8
Salads $3-4
Dinners generally $20-30
Wines from $20

You will also find impeccable presentation, warm friendly service that is both quiet and efficient, and desserts (if you can manage) that are as interesting as everything else on the menu. What you will not find are cliches.

Spencer Creek's wine list is the equal of the food, although the house selections are both reasonable and sound. Following dinner, the coffee will make you want to linger long after sunset, even on those summer nights when it's light almost to midnight Up North.

## Recipes

# Tapawingo

Here is one of those restaurants to which all food-lovers are inexorably drawn because their reputations transcend region. Some believe this is not just Northern Michigan's finest, but the state's. Pricey, yes, but all good things come dear. Pity the rich gourmand who dines there often simply because he can; better to be an infrequent but appreciative pilgrim in search of a memorable meal.

Although many of chef and owner Harlan "Pete" Peterson's dishes are richly complex and exquisite in both ingredient and preparation, Tapawingo is the essence of understated elegance. It is the product of a proprietor who is as much artist as chef. Indeed, Peterson was an automotive designer until he decided one day a dozen-odd years ago to pursue a higher calling—food.

His restaurant is a shingled cottage hidden by a tangle of shrubbery that looks out across green lawn to a little lake in the hamlet of Ellsworth. For all this charm, however, the core of Tapawingo's mystique is culinary. Anticipate a complete dining adventure, with the most meticulous attention

paid each detail.

All the sign out front says is "Tapawingo. Modern American Cuisine," which is like calling the Hope Diamond an "old stone." But it does reflect the fact that Peterson eschews the term "regional," used by so many other Northern Michigan restaurants to describe themselves. "To be a regional Michigan restaurant," he explains, "is pretty limiting in winter."

No matter how "American" Peterson chooses to be, his food is rich with international surprises. On a menu whose "principal dishes" include char-grilled beef tenderloin or pan-roasted Atlantic salmon, the appetizers may well range from Polish venison-stew to Thai-style tuna, marinated in soy, ginger and garlic and served with cabbage slaw tossed with lemon and cilantro vinaigrette.

Granted, there is usually Colorado Rack of Lamb on the menu, and Peterson acknowledges that it is something of a house specialty in many patrons' eyes. But he takes pains to explain that he does not regard it that way. "We try not to specialize," he says. "What we try to do is build this trust in people that if we have something on our menu, whatever it is, they will like it." They certainly like the lamb, which is roasted with herb-mustard crust and served with baked blue-cheese polenta.

A meal at Tapawingo is less a sequence of dishes than a culinary gestalt, a dining experience whose effect transcends description of its parts. Peterson's recipe for beef medallions, which you'll find in this book, almost makes a pleasant evening's reading all by itself. In full, it comes described as "Pan Roasted Beef Medallions With Wild Mushroom Hash and Truffled Madeira Sauce," and the ingredient he specifies for a final touch before it is borne to the dining room is "white truffle oil." Well, in testing his recipe we went 500 miles to find white truffle oil, and it was $22 an ounce. But without it, this dish is not the same. Only when that white truffle oil is added does the door open to the *sanctum sanctorum* of culinary adventure at Tapawingo.

Tapawingo's magnetism is potent. While much of the regular clientele is from nearby, especially in summer, the people at the table next to yours are equally likely to have driven from

---

## Tapawingo

9520 Lake St.
Ellsworth
616/588-7971

Dinners $28-36
Desserts $5-6
Wines from $19

---

Detroit, say, or Chicago just for a weekend built around dinner there. Any food-lover will be amply rewarded for having made the trip. Dine there once or twice and you will become a believer. Tapawingo regulars almost qualify as a sect; they subscribe to Tapawingo's newsletter, and they keep their eyes out for such feast days as annual herb luncheons and wine dinners. Atop the calendar are the "chefs' dinners' each June when Peterson's blue-ribbon colleagues from around the state and nation come to tiny Ellsworth to collaborate on a feast of feasts. Lesser mortals can themselves collaborate on the preparation of Tapawingo feasts by attending one of Peterson's hands-on cooking classes.

---

## Recipes

# Terry's Place

Terry's is a little storefront off the main drag in Charlevoix that the casual tourist might easily miss, but to knowledgeable locals it is an institution run by one of the region's hardiest restaurant veterans, Terry Left. His flagship establishment, which even the fudgies find right away, is The Villager—a spacious, family-dining pub at the corner of Bridge and Antrim Streets. Terry's Place, by contrast, is inconspicuously tucked away in a demi-basement around the corner on Antrim Street, behind a sign so low-key it easily escapes notice. Inside are a dozen-odd tables, covered by thoroughly unpretentious vinyl and surrounded by structural-brick walls adorned with Terry's wife's artwork.

Left is a local lad whose first job was washing dishes at the age of 13 at Grey Gables, a few blocks away. "I started for a dollar an hour. The Weathervane said they'd double my pay, but I was young and dumb. I said, 'I like my job. Why should I leave?' When they offered me $3.50 an hour, they hired me away." By the time he was 15, he knew he wanted to be a chef. He trained at the Culinary Institute of America and was executive chef at a five-star place in Miami before coming back home.

Terry's fare is classic French in its simplicity. His signature dish is "whitefish Grenobloise" (the recipe is in this book) and it calls for six ingredients, two of them salt and pepper; the full directions take two lines. All three recipes Left offered for this book fit on half of a sheet of paper.

Whitefish is a sort of culinary fetish with Left. He will tell you with some

pride that his three restaurants make him the biggest whitefish customer of the John Cross fishery around the corner, one of the area's biggest jobbers. Whitefish Grenobloise, he says, is the dish he would fix if the king walked in one night and asked for a dish fit for him. Talk about simple! While the fish is sautéeing, he puts a bunch of capers in a pan with butter, lemon juice, parsley and shallots, and when the butter melts, he pours it all over the fish.

The basic influence may be French, but Terry's also has an array of pasta dishes, including a glorious shrimp pasta Provençal, and all his fresh-water fish—whitefish, walleye, perch—are available various ways. One, "à la Robinson," is

---

## Terry's Place

112 Antrim St.
Charlevoix
616/547-2799

Appetizers $4-6
Entrees generally $14-18
Pasta dishes $14

---

sautéed in oil with garlic and parsley, which is about as complex as the fare gets here. If you believe in simple, Terry's is the Place. A word of caution, however: If you want whatever his nightly, off-menu special is, go early. If you don't, the locals will probably have depleted the supply.

# Recipes

# The Weathervane

This architectural landmark on the banks of the Pine River in Charlevoix is one of the quirky stone buildings designed half a century ago by Charlevoix Realtor Earl Young. Like all his structures, it is made of Michigan limestone and seems to have no straight lines. Even the shingled roof resembles a gull's wing. Built on the foundations of an old gristmill, the 'Vane has a massive stone fireplace incorporating a 9-ton boulder that vaguely resembles the map of Northern Michigan. Young adorned the interior with nautical relics, and made the bar from the planks of shipwrecks. A flight down a spiral staircase takes you to a cozy room among the boulders and timbers of the original mill, which opens to a seasonal dining deck along the river.

Today, the restaurant is one of the five in the Petoskey-based Stafford's Hospitality chain. It is not a small restaurant, so don't go there expecting intimacy. At the height of the season, in fact, it can be a madhouse on busy weekends. But the staff has the routines down pat, and we've never noticed any let-down in the standards at any season.

The menu is as expansive as the restaurant, ranging widely among a dozen soups and appetizers, whitefish four ways and steaks six, more than a dozen offerings of veal, chicken, lamb, pork, shrimp, lobster and scallops, and an array of four salads to accompany them. While this is not exactly a seafood house, you'd be right if you guess that all those nautical memorabilia suggest an emphasis of sorts on things that swim. You can have your whitefish planked, broiled in citrus butter, blackened, or sautéed with bacon, tomato, mushroom and leek. Beyond whitefish lie perch, done by two simple recipes shared among sister restaurants—sautéed in butter, sherry and garlic, or deep-fried and topped with lemon-garlic butter.

The steaks are a similarly basic line-up spanning filet mignon cordon bleu with bearnaise, T-bone with fried angel-hair onion, strip sirloin with leeks and mushrooms, and . . . well, you know.

As you might have figured out by now, the Weathervane's kitchen is a somewhat conservative place that seldom strays much farther from dead center than, say, veal Boursin or sautéed scallops on pasta with pesto. But what they do, they do well, and you can depend on it. On nights when you'd rather not have to decide among six cutting-edge innovations, this is the place. You surely will find something you'd like, and you know it'll be done with that special professional spin that all the Stafford's restaurants exhibit. It's funny, sometimes, how certain little things stick in memory, but we had whitefish at the 'Vane one midwinter weeknight recently and the accompanying lemon came tied with a ribbon in a little cloth bag to keep the juice from spraying about. Such details of old-fashioned *politesse*, too labor-intensive for most restaurants these days, set old pros apart from the crowd.

## The Weathervane

106 Pine River Ln.
Charlevoix
616/547-4311

Appetizers generally $6-7
Dinners generally $15-17
Steak dinners $16-23
   (dinners include soup or salad)

Of the many places Up North that serve dinners en masse on busy summer weekends, the Weathervane is among the best. And if you have to wait a few minutes for a table, you have all that fascinating architecture and decor to amuse you.

## Recipes

# Other Seasons Other Reasons

A few years ago, during an adventuresome weekend voyage up the coast in a very small boat, we found ourselves at day's end in Charlevoix and hungry for a good dinner. Naturally we wanted a place where we'd feel comfortable in clothes that had been wadded up all day at the bottom of a duffel. Happily, around here that's not a problem but a way of life—even for folks like us who won't settle for chainburgers or generic, carry-out pizza.

People in this part of the world tend to enjoy active outdoor lives and believe that a hard day's play entitles them to a few extra calories at just those times when they'd rather not be in the kitchen themselves. That's why Northern Michigan has so many casual restaurants, and why the only problem is picking one with good food to go along with the easy atmosphere.

A slight complication, sometimes, is that all these miles of cottage-studded shoreline mean massive seasonal population swings. Many restaurants that are delights by summer close in winter for lack of customers. Although the seasonality seems to be diminishing (especially when the skiing's good) it

remains a fact of life Up North.

Regardless of season, however, there is plenty of good-but-casual dining around here, so after a smashing day of sailing or shredding, you needn't settle for McFood. Here are some ideas.

## Whitney's

This classic waterfront saloon in Charlevoix would be one of our favorites for people-watching alone, even if they didn't have oysters on the half shell and some of the best easygoing seafood around. Facing the busy harbor across Bridge Street, it is utterly informal and rich with the patina of happy use. The paneled walls are hung with nautical art and memorabilia, and the high tables up front have tall stools from which to watch

the ebb and flow of harbor and sidewalk alike. The businesslike menu includes the likes of burgers, steaks and fish, and if perch are on offer, go for them, along with slaw and fries in the classic Up North manner. Start with a few oysters from the raw bar, washed down with a draft. If you are really hungry, try Chuck Whitney's curried chicken-and-shrimp with coconut, raisins, and a lemony cream sauce. The clientele tends to be local, and Whitney's can get crowded on summer evenings. It's always a convivial crowd, however. Frankly, we prefer Whitney's in spring and fall when it's less busy and we can sit up front and watch the world go by. On weekends, Whitney's has a fine, live blues-jazz combo in port, too. *Whitney's, 305 Bridge St., Charlevoix. 616/547-0818.*

## Chef Charles

If you think you know good pizza—like, you're from New Jersey or something—we think you should keep an open mind until you've had a slice or two from Charles Egeler's tiny Chef Charles pizzeria in Elk Rapids. It's the best we've ever found in the Midwest, and is as far removed from your generic pizza-parlor stuff as filet mignon is from pot roast. The crust is crusty outside but as weightless and fluffy as a down quilt within. He tops it with both the usual and the unexpected. The tomato sauce is bright as sunlight, and there's just enough good, fresh cheese to hold everything in place. Then comes the fun

## Emerald-Isle Adventure

A lot of people come to Northern Michigan to get away from it all, but until you've been to Beaver Island, you don't really know what away from it all means. This island in the middle of Lake Michigan combines adventure, history, and warm island hospitality.

Mormons from upstate New York settled Beaver in the 19th century, and their leader, James Strang, crowned himself "king." When he was assassinated, his disciples fled. Irish immigrants followed, and their descendants give the island its Irish flavor.

Unless you have your own boat, you get there via Charlevoix. By air it's about $50 and 20 minutes each way, but the three-hour ferry ride is more of an adventure and allows you to take the mountain bike you'll want for seeing the island. (For a price, you can also take a car, or rent a jeep or 4x4 on the island.)

Lodging includes the rustic Beaver Island Lodge on the lake, and the Bluebird B&B, run by folksinger Claudia Schmidt and her agent-husband Bill Palladino. You'll find a nice meal at the lodge's restaurant and simpler fare at the Shamrock Bar in the harbor town of St. James.

For a real treat, go on November 15, the opening day of deer season, when the Shamrock hosts the local sportsman's club's annual wild-game supper. This is a bargain-priced fund-raiser for which islanders whip up interesting dishes of venison, squirrel, rabbit, caribou, elk, and raccoon.

stuff: pepperoni, sausage, olives, chunks of pepper, artichoke hearts, onion slices, whatever. He sells it by the pie or the slice, to eat in or to go, and offers some marvelously interesting salads to go with it. One is a knockout tortellini salad, and a classic, simple Mediterranean salad that's almost a lunch by itself. For all this, his pride and joy is pesto bread—and you'll be happy to know that the secret-recipe pesto sauce on it is available bottled to go. *Chef Charles, 147 River St., Elk Rapids. 616/264-8901.*

## Spencer Creek Cafe

A few years ago, it was trendy for "fine-dining" restaurants to open "bistro" style establishments where diners could enjoy the same kind of culinary excitement in more casual surroundings. One of the best examples was Spencer Creek Cafe, next door to the exquisite white-tablecloth Spencer Creek restaurant in Alden. The cafe is a two-for-one parlay, combining a seasonal resort-town cafe with a deli and wine shop called Spencer Creek Market. The cafe has easygoing salads, soups and

sandwiches in a casual, cottage setting. The deli alongside has cheeses, specialty foods and a grand selection of wines. This is a delightful place for those times when you want to go out for lunch or dinner and have out-of-the-ordinary food, but without making a production of it. *Spencer Creek Cafe, 5160 Helena, Alden. 616/331-4171.*

## River View Cafe

After a couple of false starts under various names and owners, this little cafe overlooking the Elk River in downtown Elk Rapids seems finally to have become permanent. The fare is essentially enhanced deli food, and although the menu is limited by the lack of a real kitchen on the premises, the patrons get one of the prettiest views in Michigan. The cafe looks out on the final, willow-shrouded reach of the Elk River as it empties across the sands into East Bay. It's at its very best at sunset, and on Saturday evenings from spring through fall when a jazz trio performs for diners, the dessert-and-coffee crowd, and boaters who stroll

Mama Fortuna still hold court at their table out front on occasion, but their son, Dominic, runs the place nowadays. There's a sports-bar room to the left as you enter, but the best moments are among the massive timbers of the main dining room opposite. Dominic, a man of many talents, occasionally sings in front of his house band on weekends. Our one-word suggestion here would be "mostaccioli." Give us two words, and we'd add "tiramisu" (although it is available only in summer). Busiest in summer and on snowy weekends when skiers

across the footbridge from the marina. *River View Cafe, 210 River St., Elk Rapids. 616/264-8604.*

from nearby Shanty Creek Resort invade. *Mico's, 6311 E. Torch Lake Dr., Clam River. 616/377-6171.*

## Mico's

Maybe you can make a case for the view that classic southern-Italian food doesn't quite fit in a northwoods log cabin, but don't try to argue it with any of the regulars at Mico's. Papa and

## Elk River Inn

Long favored by folks around Elk Lake, the inn is worth visiting for two delights. The first is the lovely view of the river with Elk Lake in the distance. The other is chef and owner John Reid's whitefish parmigiana, a lavish treat in which he bakes the fish under a blanket of creamy ranch dressing laced with cheese, onion and seasonings. Both are enhanced on summer evenings when the dockside dining patio and outdoor bar are in full swing. In summer you can arrive by land or water. In winter, those of us who happen to live nearby think the inn's pine-paneled bar and dining room make a pretty nice harbor of refuge when we find ourselves clueless in the kitchen after a long day's work, saying, "Ahh, let's go out." *Elk River Inn, US-31 at the bridge in Elk Rapids. 616/264-5655.*

## Resources

Folks Up North know that from June to October, they'll find the freshest local produce at farm markets and roadside stands, and some of the best are along the coast. From Traverse City to Charlevoix, US-31 is just one good market or stand after another. We stop south of Elk Rapids at Farmer White's for sweet corn, and across the road at Guntzviller's for newly picked strawberries, raspberries, blueberries or blackberries. At apple time, there's a huge variety at Good Nature Farm Market or King Orchards near Eastport. Up around Charlevoix, Elzinga's market at Atwood is a local favorite. Cider fanciers enjoy the Hitchpoint Cider Mill near Williamsburg, where they can

see the cider made in a horse-powered press. Of course, the very freshest produce you pick yourself, which is why we like to visit Karen Shaw at Barking Dog Farm on Cairn Highway in Kewadin. In season, there are fine herbs and veggies here—if you can find anyone home besides the dogs.

---

## Olympian Heights

There are all manner of delightful fairs and festivals in Northern Michigan. Locals all know that the best fireworks are at Elk Rapids' Harbor Days the first weekend in August, and that Charlevoix's Waterfront Art Fair is one of the most prestigious in the Midwest. But the hardy northern festival-goer's brightest reward each year is the Horton Bay Winter Olympics in February. Until you've been, you don't know the full dimensions of life Up North. This is a unique afternoon's worth of odd-ball competitions you'll not find anywhere else. On the Saturday of the Olympics, hundreds of otherwise rational people assemble on the frozen surface of Lake Charlevoix and pay good money to compete in such events as ice golf, turkey-curling, and the frozen-fish toss. There's frozen bowling and bobbing for apples through holes in the ice. The whole event is a fund-raiser for the Horton Bay Fourth of July Parade, another outrageously madcap event that only helps prove that the northern lights probably do affect our minds.

---

## Recipes

# Harbor Springs—
# Petoskey—Mackinac

The northwest corner of Michigan's Lower Peninsula is a study in contrasts. At its very outer tip, on bleak Waugoshance Point, it is untamed wilderness as raw as when Michigan's only inhabitants were the Ojibwas. Yet only a few miles away lie such civilized enclaves of summer-resort gentility as Petoskey and Bay View, Harbor Springs and Mackinac.

A favorite road around here, for cyclists and motorists alike, is the Shore Drive north from Harbor Springs, along forested bluffs exposed to wild autumn storms. A huge, crooked tree that once grew here guided Indians and voyageurs in their birch canoes, and the area is still known by the French name for that crooked tree: *L'Arbre Croche*.

Modern sailors on Little Traverse Bay enjoy more sophisticated aids to navigation, as well as the fine restaurants that make Petoskey and Harbor Springs popular ports of call.

In winter, skiers work up fierce appetites on the many slopes at Nub's Nob and Boyne Highlands, or on the network of cross-country trails that lace the interior of the area.

The best and most dramatic scenery in this area is up at the Straits, where local Indians say the world was reborn after The Flood. The untamed Waugoshance shoreline still guards the Straits, where the rustic cabins of Wilderness State Park are much in demand among campers, hikers and cross-country skiers. Across the Straits lies Mackinac Island, where cars are banned and people get around in such good, old-fashioned, calorie-burning ways as walking and cycling.

There is lodging a-plenty along the area's main arteries, I-75, US-31 and US-131, as well as along Harbor-Petoskey Road (M-119), the county's most urban corridor. Serious shoppers will be thoroughly at home both in Petoskey's charming Gaslight District and in downtown Harbor Springs. Both are rich in shops and boutiques, and a serious art-lover can build a powerful hunger just touring the galleries. The Crooked Tree Arts Council runs a gallery in Petoskey, and there and in Harbor Springs there are a dozen or so fine commercial galleries featuring local artists' work. Styles range from spectacular regional landscapes in colorful impressionist style to sophisticated work that transcends region.

# The Arboretum

The Arboretum is a fixture on M-119 north of Harbor Springs, a restful place where the crystalline sound of a fountain punctuates murmured conversations and diners can unwind in the company of tall plants. Like Harbor Springs itself, it is something of an anachronism, a 1960s period piece in the lime green and canary yellow of a country-club porch and all a-twinkle with fairy lights.

The Arboretum's strength is its cellar. Owner Mark Adams is a dedicated oenophile (and the northernmost of a coterie of regional chefs who call themselves "the Wine Pigs" and gather periodically in the off-season to taste, eat, and swap yarns). Happiest for the customer, all 400-odd labels on his list are available by the glass as well as bottle, thanks to a "cruvenet" system that replaces air in opened bottles with inert nitrogen so the wine will keep after it is uncorked.

The food is decidedly eclectic but dependably traditional, as you'd expect in so tradition-steeped a locale. "We try to do new things every year," says Adams, but he acknowledges that one of the reasons he has a loyal following is that resort-town regulars like to return each season to find that the locals haven't messed around with the accustomed order of things. They have their favorite foods, and it falls to such establishments as the Arboretum to provide. Among the clientele's favorites here is braised rack of lamb, a house specialty of pan-seared chops baked with carrots, shallots and leeks in white wine seasoned with rosemary, mustard and garlic. With such straightforward classics are traditions honored. The Arboretum is no culinary research lab, although you will find some interesting appetizers, such as blackened quail or a "rumaki" in which shrimp and crab supplant chicken liver and water chestnut, and Dijon hollandaise subs for soy, ginger and garlic. Among the entrees, adventurers may be attracted by the likes of "Entrecote Bastille," char-grilled sirloin with caramelized onions and hazelnuts and a spinach-horseradish pesto.

The Arboretum is at its best in summer. Although Adams periodically

entices year-rounders with wine dinners, at other times in the off-season it can be a bit disconcerting to dine almost alone in so spacious a restaurant. Still, when snow is piled up around the picture windows, the summery atmosphere inside can kindle memories of July nights when a pianist is playing old Broadway show tunes for appreciative resorters. (Whatever the season, diners like to linger here because of the soft, cushiony leather chairs that are probably the most comfortable Up North.)

Oh, yes, there's one more thing to mention before we take leave of the Arboretum, as clinching evidence that wine undergirds the soul of the place: The final entry on the menu under "Lite Entrees" is a dinner consisting of peanut butter-and-jelly sandwiches for two with a

## The Arboretum

7075 M-119, Harbor Springs
616/526-6291

Appetizers $6-8
Dinners generally $17-20
(include soup or salad)
Lamb $24
Extensive wine list, glass or bottle

bottle of Dom Perignon, for $100. What that says about either the restaurant or its old-guard, resort-town clientele is open to debate, but whether or not anyone ever actually orders PB&J and Dom P., the mere possibility of doing so betrays a certain appreciation on the part of each of the sensibilities of the other.

# Recipes

# Andante

A few years ago, in the course of researching a story about a day in the life of a chef, we spent hours here in Bob Stark's kitchen. We had planned to spend time in several restaurants, but one day with Stark persuaded us we had no need to go anywhere else because Bob Stark is the complete chef. When it comes to designing, preparing, and serving exquisite meals, his charming restaurant is one of the three or four best Up North.

Our day with Stark began at 8 a.m., making bread for the evening to come, and ended when the last order of barbecued duck breast and Acadian peppered shrimp had been dispatched to the dining room more than 12 hours later. In between lay the preparation of sauces, the marinating of meats, the seasoning of soups, and even some crisis shopping for missing ingredients. In his tiny kitchen, Stark was an artist in the studio, and little mattered but the work at hand. At moments, all seemed to teeter on chaos and there was a constant air of quiet haste. But the focus was intense, and from his station at the stove Stark was utterly absorbed and in total charge. He not only assembled every plate, he knew

what table it was going to and sometimes knew the diner by name and preference. He checked every returning plate to assess patrons' reactions, held *sotto voce* consultations with servers, and exchanged occasional wry jibes with kitchen staff. But he never lost track of the details of each table's meal, or of the progress of the various delicacies of beef, veal, game, and fish scattered among the sauté pans, grill and ovens. Here, plainly, was a master at work.

Through it all, we knew from pleasant experience that out in Andante's quiet dining room an elegant calm prevailed. Muted conversations murmured softly on a foil of classical music and impressionist paintings, and dinner was punctuated by the gentle clink of silver and the twinkle of lights from the far shore of Little Traverse Bay. Andante, in an unpretentious house on the edge of Petoskey's

downtown Gaslight District, is a sanctuary where the food-lover can find respite from the ordinary.

Here is where the whitefish will not simply be sautéed or broiled, but baked inside a lovingly formed potato crust and served with a savory Gewurztraminer butter. Bob Stark is attuned to the culinary world around him, and strives to stay on the cutting edge. He is fond of definite flavors, so you'll find he finishes his butternut squash bisque with apple-smoked bacon, and steeps the salmon of his gravlax appetizer in coriander, Cognac and allspice and serves it on pineapple with a mustard-chive sauce.

Here is where you will find char-grilled venison on spaetzles with a luxurious Portobello mushroom sauce, or veal chops seasoned with a barbecue rub, char-grilled and served with chili and grits bearing the nutty flavor of grated Asiago cheese. The flavors sing out with Gorgonzola and Brie, chorizo and andouille, chipotle and jalapeño.

The wine list is extensive, solid, and gratifyingly far-ranging in its geography—from the Moselle and the Rhone to Sonoma, Santa Barbara and Old Mission Peninsula. And the service is the equal of

---

## Andante

321 Bay St., Petoskey
616/348-3321

Soups, Appetizers $6-8
Dinners $26-31 (include salad)
Wines $15-195 (By glass, $5-6)

---

the food and wine—refined and worldly, hospitable and attentive, knowledgeable and helpful. At Andante, recommendations are to be trusted.

You may never see the chef, but with the server as conduit, there is close communication between his corner of the kitchen and each table out front. Vacillate between two equal delights and he'll know, and may even send out a sample of whatever you didn't choose, just to see if you like it. Leave something uneaten, and there will be questions asked in the kitchen. Rave, and the chef will know it—and be pleased. Whatever you do, if you enjoy something, let your server know, because those of us who enjoy good food Up North want to keep this fellow happy in his work.

---

## Recipes

# Bay View Inn

Stafford Smith is not the sort of man you associate with empires. Gentle, unassuming, even courtly, he is right at home in the parlor of the Victorian Bay View Inn. But make no mistake, he is an emperor—the benign ruler of a domain of two hotels and five restaurants that do much to enhance life Up North. The sentimental capital of his realm is the Bay View Inn, a quaint and charming place where gentility and hospitality prevail.

The building is an unmistakeably Victorian frame structure right on the main highway through Bay View, a quaint resort town of equally antique, gingerbread cottages. Inside the inn, all is warm ambience, from the polished woodwork to the plush settees and chairs, and the flowery wallpaper soothes the soul almost as much as the friendly hospitality of the costumed, aproned waitresses who swirl so efficiently about the dining rooms. This well-trained, knowledgeable, friendly staff is a hallmark of the Stafford's Hospitality establishments.

The inn's old-fashioned charm is utterly genuine. It was built in 1886 as a rooming house, then enlarged and operated as an inn under the name Howard House. By the time Stafford Smith took a summer job as a desk clerk in the 1950s, it was the Bay View Inn. It was at the inn that Smith met his future wife, Janice, another summer worker. In 1961 they married, bought the old inn, and set about remodeling it. They added such modern touches as whirlpool bathtubs while never swerving from the Victorian when it came to decor and furnishings. It's no stretch when the company's publicity people liken it to "Great-Grandma's House," even if Great-Grandma's house didn't have 34 bedrooms.

For all the old-fashioned ambience, the kitchen is right up to date and the fare consistently, reliably good. Some of the menu is shared with other Stafford's restaurants, but much is exclusive to the Bay View Inn. Nowhere else are the brook trout baked *en papillote*, or the grilled pork chops sauced with green peppercorn cream and served

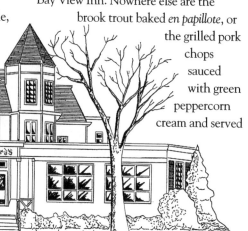

with an apple-smoked sausage. Only here are the beef tenderloin medallions dredged in peppercorns before searing, and served with a Port demi-glace and dried cherries. And only at the Bay View is that Northern Michigan menu tradition, whitefish, honored piccata-style—sautéed with mushrooms, shallots, lemon, garlic and wine. This is the home of chicken sautéed in Amaretto, and a chicken pasta with pecan-basil tomato sauce.

As you would expect, there is also much here to make the traditionalist comfy and cozy. There are baked escargots and shrimp cocktail, cold cherry soup and Great Lakes chowder, broiled whitefish and rack of lamb, and marvelous Granny Smith pies. The inn even devotes a weekend each January to live traditional jazz (a weekend, we hasten to add, when the menu is Cajun). There's more jazz each July 4 at a picnic on the lawn.

The Bay View is especially beloved among resorters around the shores of Little Traverse Bay for its monumental Sunday brunches, with everything from freshly baked waffles to roasts that are

---

## Bay View Inn

613 Woodland Ave., Petoskey
616/347-2771

Dinners generally $16-21
  (includes soup or salad)
Appetizers $5.50-7.50
Soups $3, salads $4.50

---

carved and served by the owner-host himself.

Not only can you enjoy fine food at Bay View Inn, but thanks to a peculiarity of locale, you can enjoy whatever wine you want, provided only that you bring it with you. This is because the community of Bay View is a church-affiliated association whose rules bar the sale of alcohol. The inn has no bar, no lounge, and no wine list. But there seems to be a sort of unspoken understanding, and if a guest should happen to bring a bottle of wine, the staff always manages, somehow, to provide appropriate wine glasses—perhaps from somewhere up in Great-Grandma's attic.

---

# Recipes

# The New York

There's no missing The New York in Harbor Springs, its prominent, classic, orange-brick Victorian building at Bay and State streets opposite the harbor. Owner-chef Matt Bugera aptly describes it as "an American bistro." It certainly isn't a fancy place, although it does sport a certain *fin-de-siècle* elegance, with etched-glass accents, brass fixtures, stamped-tin ceiling and rich, dark woodwork. It's the perfect companion for all those stately Victorian "cottages" that rise majestically along the shore in the posh enclaves of Harbor Point and Wequetonsing nearby.

The friendly staff is in no way formal or stuffy, and you can trust their recommendations because they know the food, which is as American as the place and runs from burgers to rack of lamb. Indeed, it was a server who first put us on to Matt's char-grilled sturgeon. Now, there's an adventure in regional cuisine for you. These ancient fish were once plentiful in Northern Michigan, and anglers still occasionally bring one up through winter ice on Black and Mullet lakes. Matt's, however, come from the Pacific Northwest, where they're pond-raised. Sturgeon is so unusual on modern menus that, says Matt, "A lot of people don't know you can eat them." Behind all that scaly armor, however, there's a delicacy, as you'll know when you try Matt's version. He grills the sturgeon as steaks and serves it with a piquant tomato-horseradish sauce.

If The New York has a signature dish, Matt says, it is "Wolverine pork loin," stuffed with cherries and wild rice. Then, too, he adds in almost the same breath, maybe it's smoked whitefish ravioli. Matt's menu is as wide-ranging as it is inventive.

The New York is a family operation. Matt's father, Bill, a retired AT&T

executive from downstate, watches the front of the house while Matt is backstage performing feats of magic he learned at the Culinary Institute of America. Matt and his wife moved north in 1983 and opened the Harbor Springs Gourmet, a deli next door on State Street. Back then The New York was known mainly for breakfasts and lunches. The Bugera family bought the restaurant in 1989, however, and transformed it, and the main event these days is dinner. The New York still does lunch, of course, and in summer you can even get breakfast if you wait until the decent hour of 10 o'clock for what Matt calls a "resort breakfast." Let us suggest that if you find yourself there at that hour, you begin your meal with one of The New York's knockout Bloody Marys. If you're not up to bloodys at that hour, the mix is sold to go for when you are.

In the evenings, families and reclusive types gravitate to the larger tables and booths up in back. The middle part, by the bar, is more tavern-like and informal. We prefer the elegant front room, with its white tablecloths and bright windows overlooking the street corner. We enjoy arriving early on a summer evening, so we can observe all the sun-bronzed resorters in transit from afternoons of play to convivial evenings of cocktails, dinner

## The New York

Bay & State Sts., Harbor Springs
616/526-6285

Entrees generally $12-15
Appetizers $5-7, soups $3-4
Salads $3.50-10

and lively conversation about spinnakers, niblicks, and backhands.

In summer, of course, you'd best book ahead, because Harbor Springs is crowded and The New York fills early. Off-season, things slow down, and year-rounders turn The New York into something of a local club. The cognoscenti look for such interesting off-season events as monthly wine-tasting dinners, January's wild-game supper, and Matt's annual Mardi Gras party.

To our minds, this is one of the top eight or ten restaurants in Northern Michigan. We especially enjoy it at Christmas time for a late lunch in the middle of a day of shopping, or for a long-drawn-out dinner in summer after a day's cycling along the shore of Little Traverse Bay or browsing all the art galleries that have appeared in Harbor Springs in the last few years.

## Recipes

# Stafford's Pier

What better place for a restaurant in a harbor town than the harbor? No wonder so many people are attracted to The Pier's Pointer Room, overlooking the busy docks and moored yachts. Once, in fact, the site literally was a harbor. The Pier's main dining room, a few steps up from the lounge and overlooking the water, is above what originally was the boathouse for a motor launch that carried passengers to and from the palatial "cottages" across the bay in the exclusive resort enclave of Harbor Point. The dining room takes its name from that vessel, the *Pointer*.

The Pier has a distinctively resort-town atmosphere, with emphasis on the yachting traditions. There is summertime service on what is known as "Dudley's Deck," which is practically part of the docks, and varnished yachting paraphernalia is visible everywhere.

The somewhat traditional menu plays well in a town to which some summer-cottage families have been returning for four or five generations in the certain expectation that things will be exactly as they left them the year before. But there

are surprises, too, for food-loving adventurers. The fare leans, appropriately enough, toward seafood, although that is by no means the sum of it. Whitefish, of course, is atop the list. The Pier offers it baked with citrus butter, char-grilled with smoked-whitefish butter, and sautéed in butter, white wine, lemon, shallots and capers. Here you will also find perch, prepared by a recipe shared with other Stafford's restaurants: rolled in seasoned flour, flash-fried and finished in a sauté pan with sherry, garlic and butter.

While grazers might not feel at home among the appetizers, traditionalists will be ecstatic. The list ranges from escargots and oysters Rockefeller to bluepoints and shrimp cocktail. There are even garlicky fried frog legs.

There is a gratifying array of landlubbers' fare as well, including beef, lamb, veal, and chicken—the latter sometimes atop a bed of morel-sauced pasta. And talk about tradition: You might even find liver with onions and bacon on the menu, although they add a

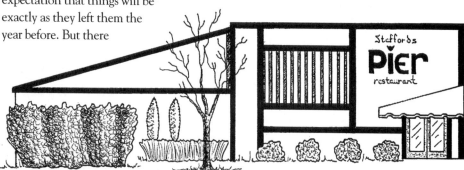

Grand Marnier sauce to convey at least a sense of uncharted waters.

Understatement counts for much in old-family resort towns, and that may help explain why something described rather casually on the menu as "Dijon mustard sauce" actually is a *duxelles* of onions and mushrooms, deglazed with sherry and reduced until almost dry, then added to a reduction of heavy cream and enhanced with two mustards. The kitchen, knowing it has a good thing on its hands, applies this delight in various ways, so you never quite know where it will show up. One night it's on sautéed chicken breast, the next on veal medallions or beef tenderloin.

The service, of course, bears the stamp

---

## The Pier

102 Bay St., Harbor Springs
616/526-6201

Appetizers $6-8
Dinners generally $17-20
(includes salad or soup)

---

of cheerful professionalism that marks all Stafford's properties. And while the Pointer Room is the main event at The Pier, many locals favor the casual atmosphere of the more informal Chart Room, a bistro-like place you'll find belowdecks, alongside a restful, easy-chaired cocktail lounge.

## Recipes

# Rose Room, Perry Hotel

One reason that no Christmas season is complete for us without a pilgrimage to Petoskey is Stafford's Perry Hotel. What a delight it is to end a day of shopping in the Gaslight District with a cocktail by the fire in the lobby lounge, followed by dinner in the Rose Room. The Perry bespeaks a sort of genteel elegance that all but vanished from much of the world half a century ago, and we folks Up North who treasure such things are grateful to Stafford Smith and Co. for having revived the Perry.

Another reason we enjoy this pilgrimage is that we just enjoy the Perry's Rose Room. We think it the best of the five good restaurants operated by the Stafford's Hospitality group, although we must confess we are hard-pressed to say just why. Some of our acquaintances disagree with us and prefer, say, the Bay View Inn or The Pier in Harbor Springs. Well, maybe we like the Perry simply because we are so inordinately fond of the ambience. But we think that it has to do with food, too. Granted, the five Stafford's restaurants' menus have much in common and share many recipes, and some of what you find at the Perry also makes frequent appearances elsewhere, even if under another name or a mild disguise. Among these traditional favorites are pork medallions "Northern Michigan," sautéed with apple, pear and cherries in apple-cider cream, as well as the usual grilled or broiled whitefish and a variety of steaks.

But it seems to us, too, that the Perry's chef, Shane Brown, takes an occasional risk to bring you dishes you won't find on its Stafford's sisters' menus. We recall, a while back, a whitefish, sautéed Niçoise style in white wine with shallots, capers, ripe olives, crushed tomato and

artichoke hearts. Another, more recently, was a dish of veal medallions sautéed with lemon and white wine, roasted red pepper, artichoke, basil and mushrooms.

The appetizer list, like the rest of the menu, is a mixture of tried and true items shared with other restaurants (e.g., seafood chowder, escargots, crab cakes, oysters Rockefeller), and dishes that are unique to the Perry. We remember particularly an appetizer-sized terrine of veal and apple with sweet-sour mustard and honey.

Such entries set the Perry's Rose Room off as much as the warm, rich decor lavished on the charming old hotel when it was remodeled in the early 1990s. They fit perfectly with the piano music that enhances Friday and Saturday evenings in the lounge off the lobby. Another event that makes Christmas time special at the hotel is the annual madrigal dinner in December, a five-course feast accompanied by singers in 16th-century costume.

For all its charm at Christmas,

---

## Rose Room

Stafford's Perry Hotel
Bay and Lewis Sts., Petoskey
616/347-2516

Dinners generally $16-22
    (include salad, veg, potato, rolls)
Appetizers generally $7-8
Soup about $3

---

however, the Perry is smashing in summer, too, when flowers overflow the planters on the massive verandah overlooking Pennsylvania Park, where you can enjoy lunch (and sometimes dinner) when the weather cooperates. It is in summer, especially, that dinner at the Perry evokes a gentler, faraway time when the resorters up from Cincinnati and Indianapolis would arrive each morning on the Northern Arrow, and step across the street from the station for breakfast at the hotel before heading off to their cottages.

## Recipes

# Walloon Lake Inn

We once asked David Beier, owner and chef of this charming Northern Michigan restaurant, to characterize his cuisine for us, and in reply got an anecdote as memorable as his food. It was a story about the time a famous French chef arrived in New York for a visit, and the culinary press turned out to pay obeisance. When one food writer asked the chef about new and exciting things he was doing back home at his restaurant in France, the chef replied: "I am not doing any things that are new. We are happy to keep working on the old ones and doing them right."

Walloon Lake is rich in the old things, one of which is the inn itself. Once called "Fern Cottage," it was established in 1890 and served as an inn where arriving summer resorters could stay until their nearby cottages were open and readied. Walloon Lake is rich in a literary sort of history conferred by Ernest Hemingway, who spent youthful summers on the lake and, as a young man in

nearby Petoskey, wrote of the region in his early yarns. Beier's menu nods in homage to Papa with a dish he calls "Rainbow Trout Hemingway." The recipe, which you'll find in this book, specifies browning the fish in butter, baking it, and serving it in a sauce of sautéed shallots and mushrooms laced with lemon juice and brandy.

Beier has had the inn since 1981, and admits he struggled a bit at first to introduce his style, which he describes as "very, very French, very, very simple." His food is so provincial that he calls it "rural," which fits nicely with the easy informality of a country inn. There is almost always a veal dish, whose preparation varies daily, and a satisfying soup. Wine plays a prominent role in the cuisine—chicken simmered in Rhone; beef in Madeira; duck in Burgundy.

This being Northern Michigan and all, indigenous game fish are regularly on offer as well—walleye, whitefish, trout. While some chefs regard whitefish as a regional cliche, Beier embraces it as "a good local product."

Like the chef in his anecdote, Beier does the old things very well. "Some of that history has rubbed off," he says. "We're not into the cutting-edge style. We never did a blackened dish." The inn is much like Walloon Lake itself, in that tradition counts. Combine that outlook with pine paneling, a sun-porch facade of cottage windows, and a view through a canopy of tall pines of sunsets over a placid, blue-green lake, and you have a timeless combination for resort-country dining.

While Beier's fare is now firmly rooted among the local traditions, it was not always so. Back when he took over the inn, for instance, local diners were accustomed to having their whitefish either fried or planked. "We were char-grilling whitefish and couldn't sell it to save our souls." Now, he says, they like things his way. "I changed the sauce one year," he remembers, "and people screamed."

Long gone are the days when the Walloon Lake Inn was merely a stopping-

## Walloon Lake Inn

4178 W. Walloon Lake Rd.
Walloon Lake Village
616/535-2999

Appetizers generally $4-6
Entrees generally $15-20
Desserts about $3.50

off place for summer resorters. It's open the year around now, seven days a week, although the hours are a bit shorter in winter. It is still an inn, however, with five cozy, heated rooms upstairs and continental breakfasts in the morning as good as the dinner the night before.

Knowledgeable year-rounders keep an eye out for periodic special events, such as cross-country ski buffets and off-season theme dinners of cuisine from a particular region—Provence, say, or Germany. Beier does a *prix fixe* Valentine's dinner, too, and a few times each year conducts one-day and four-day cooking schools (the latter make use of those rooms upstairs for pupils who wish to board).

# Recipes

# American Spoon Foods

Whenever we want to give distant friends a gift with a bit of Northern Michigan in it, we include along with the Petoskey stones and dried cherries some preserves or unsweetened "Spoon Fruit" from Petoskey-based American Spoon Foods. Our foodie friends invariably write back to ask where to get more, so we send along a catalog, but we also suggest they check their local deli or gourmet store. American Spoon's products, it seems, are sold wherever food-lovers shop.

This fascinating, success-story company was built to prominence by a Detroit grocer's son who got his start selling berries and morels by the roadside near his family's summer place outside Indian River. That would be Justin Rashid, who went big-time in 1981 in partnership with a chef in New York named Larry Forgione, to whom he had been selling morels for a restaurant specializing in "authentic American" fare. Forgione brought recipes and technical expertise to the table, and one good thing led to another. Now American Spoon Foods sells $6 million a year worth of preserves, dried fruits, veggie dips, marinades, dressings and salsa, wholesale, retail and by mail-order.

American Spoon retail outlets Up North are in Traverse City, Petoskey, Charlevoix, Harbor Springs and at Grand Traverse Resort in Acme. *American Spoon Foods, PO Box 566, Petoskey, MI, 49770; 800/222-5886.*

## Recipes

# Other Seasons
# Other Reasons

For some reason, the farther north you get in Northern Michigan, the dressier mealtimes seem to be. Why, when a fellow gets all the way up to that quaint redoubt of olden times, Mackinac Island, he can't even enter the Grand Hotel dining room without a coat and tie. Yes, these northernmost of our Up North communities are quite sophisticated, especially when it comes to food, wine, and the other hedonistic arts.

But even in these sophisticated parts the woods are thick in both summer and winter with people bent on having a good time doing things that mess up hair and devastate clothes. In summer it's hiking and biking, sailing and golf; in winter it's skiing—or just coping with snow. Consequently, folks around here are quite keen on informality. Some people, we hear, visit the area without even *bringing* a tie.

Happy to say, our hospitality industry is very accommodating, and all these towns not only offer sophistication but ample opportunities, too, for chowing down without dressing up. You don't have to go home, shower and shave and shampoo and

get out the Giorgio Armani to enjoy truly good food.

Alas, while the terrain is overrun in summer with city folks seeking respite from the world of suits, in winter it's a different story. Only the skiers and die-hards remain, so a great many fine restaurants around here are seasonal—even the grand old Grand. Another winter phenomenon the visitor should know about is the restaurateur who opens on weekends for the ski crowd, but goes snowmobiling or something from Monday to Thursday. Again, we urge you to call to be sure before you go.

Here are some suggestions for casual and seasonal dining in and around Petoskey, Harbor Springs and Mackinac.

## Crow's Nest

First-timers will need a sense of adventure for this place, at a lonely, rural crossroads

20 minutes north of Harbor Springs. It doesn't get a lot of walk-in business, and unless you live in the neighborhood dinner is best tied in with something else. We enjoy going there after a day of hiking Wilderness State Park, an autumn bike ride through the famous Tunnel of Trees, or a winter afternoon on the slopes at Nub's or Boyne. Remote location, perhaps, but vast numbers of people find their way there, summer and winter, and there's a keen sense of community about the place. Proprietor Mike McElroy is known for supporting such local causes as the school ski team, the fire department and Hospice. His place is a sort of Up North version of an English country pub. Folks from miles around chat over a pint and a meal and catch up on the kind of news CNN doesn't cover—the neighbor's new baby, say, or the barn down the road that was hit by lightning. This all happens over food ordered from a blackboard the servers haul from table to table. The Crow's Nest is not about haute cuisine, but about such venerable favorites as whitefish, lamb, steak, pan-fried walleye, and barbecued ribs. Mike does big business in pizza, too. Food, drinks and wine are priced reasonably enough that

you'll have change left over for a small contribution to one of those good causes. *Crow's Nest, 4601 N. State Rd., Cross Village. 616/526-6011.*

## The Thrill of the Hunt

One of our happiest moments as oenophiles was the time a few years ago that we found a bottle of Château Rayas 1983 *Réservé* Châteauneuf-du-Pape in the bargain bin at Symons General Store in Petoskey. Plainly, we figured, at something like $9.99 it was either a monumental labeling error or a bottle of vinegar. A few evenings later, we enjoyed one of the most astonishing red wines of our lives—rich with a soft nose, a gently buttery taste as voluptuous as a warm, hazy summer day, and a long, smooth finish. We return to Symons often, hoping lightning will strike twice. It hasn't. But we know a store that sells good stuff when we see one, and so have spent enough on lesser wines and other treats to make up to them for our jackpot. *Symons General Store, 401 E. Lake St., Petoskey, 616/3472438.* For produce, of course, the place in Petoskey is Oleson's supermarket. Even chefs shop there. Foodies for miles around were bereft a year or so ago when the store burned to the ground. But they rebuilt it almost exactly as before, crowded aisles and all, and everyone's smiling again. *Oleson's, 1050 Bayview Rd., Petoskey. 616/347-2510.*

## Carriage House

To our minds, this is Mackinac Island's finest restaurant, a genteel but relaxed waterfront hideaway tucked in behind the charming old Hotel Iroquois, of which it is the dining room. It offers fine food in intimate, summery surroundings that include a wide-window view of the

Straits. The fare is fresh and imaginative and alive with interesting combinations. The broiled whitefish is done with simple elegance, flavorful but not overwhelming, and if you want riches, there is always chef Phil Kramer's fettucine Alfredo with morels. Like practically all else on Mackinac, the Carriage House is seasonal and enjoys a bright, friendly, well-drilled young staff on the verge of degrees in psych, poli-sci, and English lit. Reservations are a good idea in high season, for the Carriage House is popular among resorters, cottagers and vacationers seeking relief from the throngs of day-trippers in pursuit of fudge and snapshots. If you have to wait for a table, it's no matter, because a delightful lounge lies just inside the street entrance, which is reached by a landscaped brick walk alongside the old hotel. The requisite bicycle rack lurks nearby, of course. *Carriage House, Hotel Iroquois, Main Street, Mackinac Island. 906/847-3321.*

## Grand Hotel

No restaurant in Northern Michigan (or anywhere, for that matter) is quite like the main dining room of the Musser family's Grand Hotel. Dinner here is equal parts food, tradition and theater—a mealtime pageant with the diners as part of the cast. This is the only place Up North where one is still expected to dress for dinner, and gentlemen must wear coat and tie (for that rule alone, the Mussers are to be commended). New arrivals promenade down the long, central aisle of the cavernous dining room, as much on display as models on a runway. On either side, among the orderly rows and ranks of tables, well-drilled teams of uniformed Jamaican waiters swarm and hover, bearing course after course with happy precision. For a restaurant that serves whole legions at a sitting and is open but five months a year, the food is predictably good. Grand Hotel service has unmatched panache, and the setting is unequaled in all the world. Dining room patrons who are not guests in the hotel pay a fixed price ($50 at last look) that seems steep until you realize you'd pay at least as much anywhere else for dinner and theater tickets to a show this good. Before dinner, be sure to have cocktails in the hotel's rooftop piano bar with a breath-takingly panoramic view of the Straits. *Grand Hotel, Grand Ave., Mackinac Island. 906/847-3331.*

## Douglas Lake Bar

Here's a charmer tucked away in so remote a corner of Emmet County that the casual tourist might never find it. That may be just as well in the eyes of knowing locals and veteran resorters, who flock to their beloved DLB on summer eves for some of Hoot Rudolf's lovingly prepared steak or walleye. That's only part of the story, of course; you'll also find excellent veal, perch, whitefish and pasta. Ambience-wise, the DLB is a Northwoods classic—dark paneling, stone fireplace, antlered trophy, and a screened porch overlooking the lake. It's so rustic, it can deceive the newcomer. On our first visit, we went expecting burgers and enjoyed instead the best steak au poivre we can recall—butter-tender filet mignon, charred to a light crust outside, molten pink within, and sauced with a light Dijon and Cognac cream. This was just the thing to wash down with something from a short but solid wine list. Regulars may hate us for telling you, but you'll find it two miles east of US-31 on Douglas Lake Rd., which turns off opposite the Pellston Airport. *Douglas Lake Bar & Steakhouse, 7314 Douglas Lake Rd., Pellston.* 616/539-8588.

## Noggin Room

You hardly ever hear the word "rathskeller" any more, but if you know anyone too young to have heard it at all, here's the place where you can show them one. The Noggin Room defines the word. A dimly-lighted tavern in the cellar of Petoskey's beautifully remodeled old Perry Hotel, it's just the place for a cup of chowder or a burger, which you can wash down with one of 30-odd imported beers from England, Germany, China,

Czechoslovakia, Poland, Australia, Mexico, Holland, Ireland, Jamaica and Canada. The fare is soup, salads, pizza and burgers (and nachos, which we admit smacks more of a cantina than a rathskeller, especially if you wash it down with a Dos Equis). Many Petoskey year-rounders and Bay View cottagers consider this their "local" when they want a casual night out. *Noggin Room, in Stafford's Perry Hotel, Bay and Lewis Sts., Petoskey. 616/347-2516.*

## Roast and Toast

Every town needs a place where shoppers and business people can go for a quick, light, fresh, delicious and polyunsaturated lunch. That is to say, every town needs a Roast and Toast. At the moment, only Petoskey has one, however, so that's where you want to be when you're Up North and find yourself craving something simple and honest in the middle of a hard day's shopping. Roast and Toast's Bob and Mary Keedy have married the fine art of fast, efficient friendly service to the happy science of savory, homemade soups and fresh and interesting salads. As a bonus, they roast their own world-class coffee right on the premises. You'll find two or three soups every day from an ever-changing list

that frequently includes tomato-herb minestrone, potato and leek, lemony-spinach and black bean. Nothing humdrum here. The sandwich and salad menu is more fixed, but encompasses all the favorite deli stuff, from ham and Swiss to turkey and provolone. Our personal favorites are grilled-chicken Caesar salad and a romaine salad with pecans, blue cheese and a homemade vinaigrette. Best of all, Bob bakes the breads, brownies and cookies fresh every day, along with the bagels, Danish and muffins he has ready each morning for the bleary-eyed when Roast and Toast opens for breakfast. *Roast and Toast, 309 E. Lake St., Petoskey, 616/347-7767.*

## Juilleret's

Five generations of Juillerets have operated the family place, which is such a Northern Michigan landmark that the present Juilleret, Jim, claims his ancestors invented planked whitefish. The Indians might beg to differ, but who's to say?

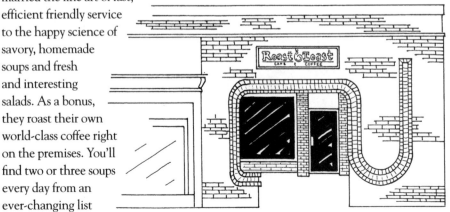

## The Sweet Life

We Northerners sometimes refer to our summer visitors as "fudgies," a term of endearment born of tourist tastes that a lot of us locals share. A doctor friend once theorized that fudge is big Up North because our systems crave sweets in winter. That might explain why we make maple sugar in March, but it hardly explains why fudgies buy fudge in July. Nowhere do they buy as much of it as on Mackinac, where the aroma of fudge-in-the-making is sometimes strong enough to make you forget how many horses there are on the island.

Fudge is brand new compared to maple syrup and sugar. Maple sugar predates history. Ojibwas celebrated spring by moving from their winter camp to their "sugarbush," or maple grove. When white traders and settlers showed up, they were hooked the moment they tasted maple sugar. In 19th-century Mackinac, the first sign of sap sent the entire island off in sleighs across five miles of ice to Bois Blanc Island. There, everyone tapped maples and boiled sap by day, and partied down by night. The sugaring lasted three weeks or until all the single folks were paired off, whichever came first. Then, as now, the islanders had more in mind than feeding their own sweet tooth. They sold their maple sugar as far away as Chicago, St. Louis and New York.

Juilleret's goes back almost as far as they do. The original place, more than a century ago, was an ice-cream parlor whose counter was a pine plank on sawhorses. Over the years it grew into a restaurant, and during Prohibition was briefly a dance hall. With the return of booze it became a restaurant again, but in 1960 they dropped the drinks and returned part way to their roots, becoming a family restaurant and ice cream parlor. They make their own ice cream and root beer, and offer a whole menu for all three meals, from fluffy breakfast waffles or cinnamon French toast to homemade soup, salads, sandwiches and of course, planked whitefish. All this comes in a bright, busy, family atmosphere. This is one of the few places where an old-timer can order a club sandwich and a chocolate soda and get something recognizable as such. The house specialty dessert is the famous "velvet," a silky concoction of ice cream, chocolate and marshmallow. But you can't have one in January, because this is strictly a seasonal establishment. *Juilleret's. 131 State Street, Harbor Springs, 616/526-2821.*

## Recipes

# Chefs' Cookbook

In the course of talking to Northern Michigan chefs for this book, we have amassed what we think is an interesting collection of recipes that fairly represent the styles, scope and inventiveness of the region's restaurants. We asked each chef to contribute a menu of recipes typical of their kitchen's product. Some of them did exactly that. Others (being Northern Michiganders) chose to go their own ways and offered assortments of their own choosing that don't necessarily constitute a "menu." A few contributed just one or two dishes, a few contributed half a dozen or more, and some offered us virtually unrestrained access to their entire libraries.

Almost all the full-service, year-round restaurants have at least one recipe somewhere in this book, as do many specialty and seasonal restaurants. As far as we can tell, all the recipes are for dishes you'll find on the restaurants' menus at least some of the time, if not daily. We make no guarantees in this regard, however, because menus (and styles) change. We have been collecting material for this book for nearly two years, and in that much time whole culinary trends can come and go. By the time you read this, some of our restaurants may sport entirely new menus. Moreover, we made it clear to all the chefs that the recipes did not have to be something they offer regularly (or even at all), so long as they fairly represent their restaurant's styles.

You will find some sorts of dishes represented more frequently than others. Predictably enough, for instance, that Northern Michigan staple, whitefish, appears often. You'll find it smoked, grilled, baked, sauteed, and made into chowder. More than a few chefs offered dishes involving morels, another regional delicacy. Fruits grown in Northern Michigan also figure prominently, from raspberries and strawberries to cherries and apples. Northern Michigan's chefs have plenty of adventure in their souls, however, and their recipes reflect ample influence from faraway places. All the great fashions of recent years appear, including Thai, Cajun, Provençal, Tex-Mex, and *la nouvelle cuisine*. As you'd expect, there is no small amount of classic French accent in here as well. (One thing you'll not find is a recipe for "tall" food, the latest fashion among chefs on the East and West coasts. It hasn't made it to the North Coast, but that may be only a matter of time.)

We have included several of our own recipes. After all, we reasoned, if we ask all these chefs to tell us their secrets, the least we can do is offer a few in return. Although these include a couple of beefy items (and a smashing pork barbecue from brother Phil in Quincy, Illinois), you'll find that our recipes lean towards seafood and salads. We seem to have collected a lot of fish recipes because we catch a lot of fish in this part of the world, and so are constantly on the lookout for new and different things to do to them. Please note that any recipe for freshwater lake fish probably would work equally well for one as another—whitefish, bass, walleye, perch, or whatever you caught today.

Our original thought about recipes was that we would simply collect them from our various chefs, type them up and publish them. We soon realized, however, that we would have to be considerably more cautious than that. No matter how skilled they are in the kitchen, chefs can be quite vague when it comes to putting it in writing. They sometimes forget, for instance, to mention crucial steps because they take them for granted, or specify a baking temperature because they simply keep such data in their heads. Quantities posed problems, too. We found it is not always easy to take the ingredients for, say, eight gallons of chowder and translate them to "serves 6." We learned early on that we would have to test any recipes about which we had any doubts. So we enlisted an army of volunteer testers, who did noble service in our cause. Their names are listed here, and we publicly thank them all for their efforts and their thoughtful comments.

We also thank the chefs and proprietors who have allowed us to publish what are, essentially, trade secrets—their recipes. We did not use all the recipes offered us. In a few cases this was because they did not translate well for small quantities, but mostly it was simply to avoid repetition. At one point, for instance, we had six recipes for crab cakes, and we decided that was about four too many. We are grateful, however, even for recipes we did not use.

For all our testing, we realize that errors remain not only possible but likely. If any recipe in this book lets you down, we ask that you do two things: First, forgive us. Second, let us know (you'll find our address in the front of the book) so we can correct the problem in future editions.

— SDeC / GDeC

# Connoisseur Up North Recipe-testing Panel

Meredith BeVier, Traverse City
Maria and Pat Bonadeo, Petoskey
Carolyn Burch, Elk Rapids
Cheryl Ferguson, Traverse City
Maureen D'Avanzo, Northville
Kay Grady, Seattle
Rose Hollander, Suttons Bay
Cheryl Humbarger, Battle Creek
Harry Jarboe, Neahtawanta
Tom Kachadurian, Traverse City
Charles Kralovec, Chicago
Susan Lanciault, Bloomfield Hills
Kelly O'Hara, Suttons Bay
Nancy Powell, Old Mission
Harry Santen, Cincinnati
Marilyn Schlack, Kalamazoo
Karen Shaw, Kewadin
Linda Stafford, Greenville
Marilyn Summerfield, Elk Rapids
Dave & Lisa Taylor, Traverse City
Deb and Nick Taylor, Williamsburg

# Appetizers

## Andante
# Louisiana Crab Cakes
with Chipotle Mayonnaise

*(Serves up to 12 as appetizer)*

### CRAB CAKES

| | | | | |
|---|---|---|---|---|
| 1 lb | blue lump crab meat | | 2 t | dry mustard |
| 1/4 t | cayenne | | 2 t | Worcestershire sauce |
| 2 | eggs | | 1/2 C | tartar sauce |
| 1/2 C | bread crumbs | | 2 T | clarified butter |

Carefully pick over crab meat to remove any bits of shell. Combine with remaining ingredients. Shape into cakes and fry in clarified butter until golden. Serve with chipotle mayonnaise (below).

### CHIPOTLE MAYONNAISE

| | | | | |
|---|---|---|---|---|
| 3 | egg yolks | | 4 | garlic cloves |
| 1/4 C | lemon juice | | 2 t | cumin |
| 2 t | chili powder | | 2 T | chipotle chili |
| 1 C | olive oil | | | salt, cayenne pepper to taste |

Place all ingredients except oil into bowl of a mixer, and with machine running, slowly drizzle in the oil so mixture emulsifies. Season to taste.

Arboretum

# Grilled Portobello Mushroom Caps
With Basil and Aged Provolone

*(Serves 4)*

| | | | | |
|---|---|---|---|---|
| 1/2 C | butter | | 1/4 C | chopped fresh basil |
| 1 T | chopped fresh garlic | | 4 | Portobello caps |
| 1 C | grated, aged provolone | | | salt and pepper to taste |

Soften butter. Add garlic, basil, salt and pepper. Mix well and set aside. Cook mushroom caps on a hot grill until tender (about 5 minutes). Arrange on four plates. Heat basil butter and drizzle over mushroom caps. Finish each plate with grated provolone.

The Bluebird

# Leland Smoked Whitefish
With Norwegian Dill-Horseradish Sauce

*(Serves 8-10)*

| | | | | |
|---|---|---|---|---|
| 2 lb | smoked whitefish | | 1/4 C | horseradish (drained) |
| 1 t | sugar | | 1/4 t | lemon juice |
| 1/2 t | fresh ground black pepper | | 2 t | dry dill weed |
| 1 C | sour cream | | | |

Mix sauce ingredients well and spoon over fish, or serve on the side in a bowl. Garnish plates with lemon slices.

La Bécasse

# Smoked Salmon Timbales
## With Vermouth and Sorrel Sauce

*(Makes 6 timbales)*

## TIMBALES

| | | | |
|---|---|---|---|
| 24 | spinach leaves, blanched | 1 t | butter |
| ³/₄ lb | boneless smoked salmon | 4 | shallots, minced |
| ³/₄ C | cream | 4 | eggs |
| pinch | tarragon | pinch | white pepper |
| 2 t | lemon juice | | |

Butter six timbale molds or custard cups (you can use no-stick spray instead) and line with blanched spinach leaves. Combine salmon, shallots, cream, eggs, tarragon, pepper, and lemon juice and puree in food processor. Divide among the lined molds and cover with aluminum foil. Tap each mold on the counter to remove air bubbles, then bake in a water bath at 300ºF for 40 minutes or until knife inserted in center comes out clean. Turn timbales out of molds and garnish with:

## VERMOUTH AND SORREL SAUCE

| | | | |
|---|---|---|---|
| 2 | shallots, minced | 2 T | butter |
| ¹/₂ C | dry vermouth | ¹/₄ C | cream |
| 1 t | lemon juice | 2 T | finely sliced sorrel |

Saute shallots in butter until tender. Deglaze pan with vermouth. Stir in cream, lemon juice and sorrel. Reduce until thickened.

Hattie's

# Smoked Whitefish Cakes
## With Tomato Butter Sauce

*(Serves 8)*

### TOMATO BUTTER SAUCE

| | | | |
|---|---|---|---|
| $3^1/_4$ T | olive oil | $1^1/_4$ | carrots |
| $^2/_3$ | small red onion | 1 stalk | celery |
| 1 | lg garlic clove | 4 C | plum tomatoes, chopped |
| $^3/_4$ C | chicken stock | $^2/_3$ C | dry white wine |
| $^1/_8$ | red bell pepper, crushed | $1^1/_4$ | bay leaves |
| $^3/_4$ t | salt | $^1/_3$ t | pepper |
| $^2/_3$ t | oregano | dash | basil |
| dash | thyme | | |

Saute carrot, onion, celery and garlic in olive oil. Add tomatoes and simmer 10 minutes. Add remaining ingredients and simmer 20 minutes or until thickened.

### SMOKED WHITEFISH CAKES

| | | | |
|---|---|---|---|
| 2 lb | smoked whitefish | $2^1/_3$C | mashed potatoes, cooled |
| $^3/_4$ C | diced celery | $^3/_4$C | chopped onion |
| $^3/_4$ | red pepper, chopped | $2^1/_3$t | clarified butter |
| $2^1/_3$t | tarragon | $1^1/_4$t | salt |
| $^3/_4$ C | breadcrumbs | $^3/_4$ t | pepper |

Bring smoked fish to room temperature. Thoroughly skin, bone and pin-bone fish. Saute peppers, onion and celery in clarified butter until tender. Combine all ingredients except breadcrumbs in a bowl and let cool. Form into patties, coat with crumbs and saute in clarified butter. Serve with tomato butter sauce.

Hattie's

# Thai Scallops
With Cucumber Relish

*(Serves 8)*

| | | | |
|---|---|---|---|
| ¹/₃ C | rice vinegar | ¹/₄ C | sugar |
| ¹/₄ t | red pepper flakes | ¹/₄ C | water |
| ¹/₄ | lemon, chopped | ³/₄ t | salt |
| 3 | cucumbers | 3 T | chopped cilantro |
| ¹/₄ C | lime juice | 1¹/₂ t | diced jalapeño |
| ¹/₄ C | olive oil | 4 C | scallops |

Peel and seed the cucumbers and cut into half-inch slices, dice, and place into a metal pan or bowl. In a saucepan, combine vinegar, sugar, salt, red pepper, water and lemon. Bring to a boil, stirring to dissolve the sugar, and strain, and pour the hot liquid over the cucumbers. Add the cilantro, jalapeño and lime juice. Chill overnight before serving. Saute scallops in olive oil, on medium-high heat about 1 minute a side or until lightly browned. Serve on top of relish.

Left Bank

# Sun-dried Tomato-Basil Roulades

| | | | | |
|---|---|---|---|---|
| 1 lb | cream cheese | 1 T | vodka |
| 2 t | grated lemon zest | 4 | garlic cloves, minced |
| 2 oz | sun-dried tomato, chopped | 1 pkg | lahvosh bread |
| 1/2 C | chopped roast hazelnuts | | fresh basil leaves |

Bring cream cheese to room temperature. In a bowl, cream together the cheese, vodka, lemon zest, garlic and add sun-dried tomato. Lay bread (you can use 12-inch flour tortillas instead) on a flat surface and spread with cream cheese mixture. Lay fresh basil leaves on top and sprinkle with hazelnuts. Roll the bread or tortillas tightly, mist with water, then roll each tightly in plastic wrap. Refrigerate at least one hour. Before serving, trim the ends of each roll, cut on the diagonal into 15 slices. serve slightly chilled or at room temperature.

Monte Bianco

# Pizzetta con Aglio e Cambozola

(Serves 4)

| | | | | |
|---|---|---|---|---|
| 4 | heads of garlic | 1 T | rosemary-garlic olive oil |
| 3/4 lb | cambozola cheese | | |
| 1/2 to 1 | sheet focaccia bread (depending on size of bread) | | |

Snip off the tops of the garlic heads to expose cloves. Peel the outer layers but do not expose the flesh. Brush garlic heads lightly with olive oil, place in a small, shallow baking dish and cover with foil. Roast at 325ºF until heads are soft (about 1 hour). Brush desired quantity of focaccia bread lightly with rosemary-garlic oil, and warm over grill or in oven at 350ºF for about 5 minutes. Cut cambozola into eight equal wedges. Place two slices of cheese on each plate and place under broiler until soft and bubbly. Serve cheese with heads of garlic and focaccia bread. Diners can peel garlic cloves one at a time and squeeze out flesh to spread with cheese on bread.

## The New York

# Smoked Whitefish Raviolis
#### With Tomato and Caper Cream Sauce

*(Serves 8)*

### RAVIOLI FILLING

| | | | |
|---|---|---|---|
| 8 oz | smoked whitefish | 4 oz | cream cheese |
| | fresh herbs— e.g., basil, chives, parsley, tarragon | | |

Remove skin from fish and debone. Mix cream cheese and meat, blending in herbs to taste.

### PASTA DOUGH

| | | | |
|---|---|---|---|
| 3-4 C | flour | 2 T | olive oil |
| 4 | eggs | | salt to taste |

Put 3 cups of flour in mixing bowl, form a well, and add eggs and oil and salt, if desired. Mix eggs and oil with a wooden spoon, then slowly mix into the flour. When dough comes together, put out on a well-floured surface (use reserved cup of flour) and knead until firm and smooth. Wrap tightly and refrigerate.

### TOMATO CAPER CREAM SAUCE

| | | | |
|---|---|---|---|
| 2 oz | white wine | 8 oz | heavy whipping cream |
| $^1/_2$ C | chopped fresh tomato | 2 T | capers |

Peel, seed and chop tomato. Bring wine to boil in heavy, non-corroding pan. Add tomato and cook until most of the liquid evaporates. Add heavy cream and simmer 10 minutes. Add capers.

### FINAL PREPARATION:

Roll dough in pasta machine to second thinnest setting. Place a sheet of pasta on a floured ravioli mold. Spoon in filling. Brush a second sheet with egg wash, put on top, cut with rolling pin and refrigerate on floured tray until ready to cook. Add raviolis gently to a gallon of boiling, salted water and cook about 3 minutes. Drain, place in warm bowl, and spoon on tomato-caper sauce. Sprinkle with herbs.

The New York

# Creamy Polenta
## With Morels and Chive Cream

*(Serves 6)*

| | | | |
|---|---|---|---|
| 1 oz | dried morels (or 8 oz fresh) | 4 C | chicken stock |
| 2 C | yellow cornmeal or polenta flour | | Parmesan cheese |
| 4 oz | butter | 1 oz | white wine |
| 1 T | chopped shallots | 4 oz | heavy cream |
| 1 bunch | fresh chives | | |

Soak dried morels in warm water to reconstitute. In a heavy saucepan, bring stock to boil and slowly pour in the cornmeal, stirring constantly. Reduce heat and simmer 20 minutes. (If the polenta gets too dry, add stock or water.) Stir in butter and set polenta aside. Put morels, some morel juice and the wine into a saute pan over high heat, bring to a boil and reduce until almost dry. Turn down heat, add shallots and heavy cream, and simmer until it reaches consistency of sauce. Add chives. Spoon polenta into warm bowls, top evenly with morel sauce, sprinkle with chives, and serve with freshly grated Parmesan cheese.


The Rowe

# Pecan Stuffed Morels

*(Serves 8)*

| | | | |
|---|---|---|---|
| 1 lb | morels | 1/2 C | butter |
| 1 C | chopped onion | 1 t | salt |
| 1 T | melted butter | 1/2 t | black pepper |
| 1/2 t | paprika | 5 C | dry bread crumbs |
| 1 1/2 C | coarsely chopped pecans | 1 C | chopped celery |

Clean morels, trim and set stems aside. Melt butter in large, heavy skillet and saute onion, celery and chopped morel stems until tender and transparent. Stir in seasonings, bread crumbs and pecans. Stuff morels and set with points up on a buttered baking sheet. Drizzle with melted butter and bake at 350°F for 20 to 30 minutes. Serve upright on chopped parsley or other greens.

Northern Delights

# Baba Ganouj
### With Tahini Dressing

*(Yields approx. 1 pint)*

## TAHINI DRESSING (ABOUT 3 CUPS)

| | | | |
|---|---|---|---|
| 1 C | tahini (sesame-seed paste) | $3/4$ t | cumin |
| $1/4$ t | minced garlic | 1 t | coriander |
| 1 t | dill | $1/8$ t | ground black pepper |
| 1 C | water | $1/2$ t | paprika |
| $1/3$ C | lemon juice | $1/2$ C | olive oil |
| dash | red wine vinegar | 2 T | orange juice |
| $1 1/2$ t | salt | $1/4$ C | minced parsley |

Mix ingredients thoroughly in a blender. (This will make about 3 cups; recipe below requires $1/2$ cup).

## BABA GANOUJ

| | | | |
|---|---|---|---|
| 2 | med. eggplants | 2 | lemons, juiced |
| 1/2 C | tahini dressing | $1/4$ C | finely chopped scallions |
| | salt, pepper to taste | | |

Bake eggplants at 350°F until soft, then grill over open flame until skin is charred. Scoop out flesh and discard skin. Process eggplant, tahini dressing and lemon juice until smooth. Add scallions, salt and pepper.

# On the Edge

# Spicy Shrimp
With Blue Cheese Dressing

---

SHRIMP

| | | | | |
|---|---|---|---|---|
| 16 | lg. tiger shrimp | | 6 T | paprika |
| 2 T | salt | | 3 T | garlic powder |
| 1$^1$/$_2$ T | black pepper | | 1$^1$/$_2$ T | onion powder |
| 1$^1$/$_2$ T | cayenne pepper | | 1$^1$/$_2$ T | dried oregano |
| 1$^1$/$_2$ T | dried thyme | | $^1$/$_2$ C | canola oil |

Skewer shrimp tail-first on wooden skewers. Mix dry seasonings. Coat shrimp with oil and dust with seasoning. Grill 2-3 minutes or until done (be careful not to overcook).

BLUE CHEESE DRESSING

| | | | | |
|---|---|---|---|---|
| $^1$/$_2$ T | chopped garlic | | $^1$/$_4$ C | chopped onion |
| 2 C | mayonnaise | | $^3$/$_4$ C | sour cream |
| $^1$/$_4$ C | lemon juice | | $^1$/$_4$ C | cider vinegar |
| $^3$/$_4$ lb | blue cheese | | | salt, pepper to taste |

Combine all ingredients in large bowl and mix well. (This will make more than needed for 16 shrimp.)

Spencer Creek

# Warm Leek Tart
## With Sun-dried Tomato and Brie

*(Serves 4)*

### TART SHELL

| | | | |
|---|---|---|---|
| 2 C | all-purpose flour | $^1/_2$ t | salt |
| $^1/_2$ C | diced cold butter | 3 T | chilled Crisco |
| 5-6 T | ice water | | |

Combine flour and salt, cut in butter and Crisco until mixture is pea-size granules. Add water, a tablespoon at a time, mixing by hand to form a ball. (Amount of water needed may vary.) Chill ball for 3 hours. Place chilled dough on floured board, roll to $^1/_4$-inch thickness, and place in 9-inch tart pan. Prick bottom of shell with fork. Place parchment paper inside shell and weigh down with rice. Bake at 350ºF until light, golden brown (about 15-20 minutes). Set shell aside.

### TART

| | | | |
|---|---|---|---|
| $^1/_2$ | med. red onion, sliced thin | 3 T | kosher salt |
| 2 T | olive oil | 6 oz | cream cheese |
| 2 | medium leeks | $^1/_4$ c | water |
| 1 C | packed sun-dried tomatoes | 8 oz | Brie, with paper removed |
| 1 t | balsamic vinegar | 2 | plum (Roma) tomatoes |
| 4-6 | fresh basil leaves, chopped | | |

Toss onion in kosher salt. Place in colander and let sit 1 hour. Reconstitute tomatoes and chop. Rinse onions under cold water, drain and pat dry. Slice leek white finely ($^1/_8$-inch) and saute in 1T oil until tender, then add water and cook down until water has evaporated. Let cool. In mixer, blend cream cheese, red onion and leek. Spread mixture $^1/_4$-inch thick in tart shell. Layer sun-dried tomatoes on top. Drizzle balsamic vinegar over tomatoes. Roll Brie (between two sheets of parchment paper) to diameter of tart shell and place on top of tomatoes. Bake tart at 350ºF for 5 to 7 minutes. Garnish with diced plum tomatoes tossed with fresh basil and olive oil.

Stafford's Pier

# Smoked Salmon Mousse

*(Serves 6-8)*

| | | | |
|---|---|---|---|
| 8 oz | hot smoked salmon | 16 oz | cream cheese |
| 1 T | horseradish | 2 oz | sour cream |

Combine salmon, sour cream and horseradish in processor and process until smooth.
Add cream cheese and blend until smooth. Pipe into serving dish and serve with
crackers or wafers.

Stubb's

# Grilled Shrimp and Seared Scallops
With Tropical Citrus Melon Salsa

| | | | |
|---|---|---|---|
| 12 | sea scallops | 12 | lg. shrimp (16-20/lb) |
| 1/2 C | finely diced fresh pineapple | 1/2 C | finely diced cantaloupe |
| 1/2 C | finely diced honeydew | 1 | lemon |
| 2 | limes | 1 | orange |
| 1 | red bell pepper, finely diced | 1/4 C | roughly chopped cilantro |
| 1 | jalapeño, minced | | salt to taste |

Peel lemon, orange and one lime, remove seeds and membranes, and chop. Starting with
pineapple in a bowl, add chopped citrus, juice of the other lime, melon, peppers and
cilantro. Mix thoroughly and let the flavors marry for one hour. Peel and devein shrimp.
Wash and drain shrimp and scallops. Slice each scallop in half horizontally. When ready
to serve, heat a non-stick pan over high heat until very hot, and sear scallop pieces on
both sides, doing as many at a time as comfortable and keeping the finished ones warm.
Periodically wipe the pan with a clean cloth. On the hottest part of a preheated grill,
mark the shrimp on both sides, then transfer to cooler part of grill to finish. Arrange
shrimp and scallops on plates and serve with salsa spooned alongside.

Trillium

# Wild Mushrooms
## with Angel-Hair Pasta

*(Serves 4)*

### PASTA

| | | | |
|---|---|---|---|
| 4 oz | dried angel hair (or 8 oz fresh) | 3 qt | boiling salted water |
| 1 t | chopped fresh basil | 1 t | chopped fresh oregano |
| 1 t | chopped fresh tarragon | 1/4 t | chopped fresh thyme |
| 3 T | butter | | |

Bring water to boiling, add pasta and cook until tender, stirring occasionally. Drain, add butter and chopped herbs, toss, and hold covered.

### SAUCE

| | | | |
|---|---|---|---|
| 2 T | minced shallots | 2 T | butter |
| 1 C | dry white wine | 2 C | morel juice |
| 3 C | heavy whipping cream | | |

In a 3-qt. sauce pot, saute the shallots in butter until translucent. Add wine and morel juice (from rehydrating morels; see below). Reduce by half. Add whipping cream and reduce to desired thickness. Simmer on low heat.

### MUSHROOM MIX AND PRESENTATION

| | | | |
|---|---|---|---|
| 2 C | fresh shiitakes | 2 C | fresh oyster mushrooms |
| 1 C | dried morels (soaked in 3 C water) | 2 T | minced shallots |
| 1 T | minced garlic | 3 T | butter |

De-stem shiitake and oyster mushrooms and cut larger mushrooms to bite size. Saute shallots and garlic with butter until translucent. Add mushrooms and cook until tender. Add cream sauce and cook to desired thickness. Arrange mushrooms around perimeter of plate, pour remaining sauce over them, arrange pasta in center. Garnish with a fresh herb sprig.

Walloon Lake Inn

# Pissaladiere (Onion Tart)

*(Serves 8)*

| | | | |
|---|---|---|---|
| 1 C | flour | | salt to taste |
| 10 T | butter, diced | 4 T | cold water |
| 4 T | olive oil | 2 lb | sweet onion |
| 8 | salted anchovies | 1/2 C | olives |

Make pastry of flour, salt, butter, and water, taking care not to overwork it. Form into an inch-thick block and chill in plastic wrap at least an hour. Peel and slice onions, and cook covered until semi-pureed (about an hour). Remove lid and let moisture evaporate. Roll pastry dough to 1/8-inch thickness and crimp edges. Spread onion over dough and decorate with olives and anchovies. Drizzle with oil and bake at 375°F about 30 minutes, until edges are crisp and brown.

The Authors

# Char-grilled Shrimp
With Hot Thai sauce

*(Serves 8)*

| | | | |
|---|---|---|---|
| 16 | jumbo shrimp | 1 T | curry powder |
| 1 T | olive oil | 2 T | mayonnaise |
| 1 t | nam pla fish sauce | 4 T | spicy Thai chili sauce |
| 1 t | Dijon mustard | 2 T | catsup |
| 2 t | lemon juice | | |

Peel, devein, wash and dry shrimp. Toss lightly with oil and sprinkle with curry. Mix remaining ingredients to make dipping sauce. Grill shrimp. Serve with toothpicks or skewers for dipping.

The Authors

# Lemon Smoked Whitefish Pâté

*(Serves 6-8)*

| | | | |
|---|---|---|---|
| ¹/₂ lb | smoked whitefish | 6-8 | med. shrimp, cooked |
| ¹/₂ | med. onion, finely chopped | 4-6 oz | cream cheese |
| ¹/₂ | lemon (for juice) | 1 t | curry powder |
| ¹/₄ t | anchovy paste | | |

Remove and discard fish skin and all bones, and chop flesh finely. Chop shrimp very finely. In a bowl, thoroughly mix all ingredients except lemon juice, using just enough cream cheese to bind solids. Serve patÈ on crackers, melba rounds or troweled into lengths of celery garnished with parsley. Sprinkle with lemon juice to brighten just before serving.

# Matinenda Shrimp

*(Serves 6)*

| | | | |
|---|---|---|---|
| 1 | 15-inch smallmouth, freshly caught | 2 | limes, juiced |
| ¹/₂ C | catsup | 1 T | horseradish |
| ¹/₄ t | Tabasco | ¹/₄ t | Worcestershire |
| ¹/₂ t | lemon juice | | |

Filet, skin and pin-bone fish. Inspect closely and remove any worms or parasites, then wash, pat dry, and cut into strips the size of cocktail shrimp. Cover with lime juice in a non-reactive container and marinate in refrigerator 24 hours, stirring occasionally. Drain before serving. Mix remaining ingredients to make a cocktail sauce. Serve as you would shrimp cocktail. (*This ceviche is a summer appetizer for the angler in need of something new to do with all those fish. It's named for the Canadian lake that provides most of our bass. Any other fresh fish will do. For variety, spice the marinade with onion, tomato, garlic, ginger, curry or peppers.*)

# Soups

Arboretum

# Roasted Red Bell Pepper Soup
With Rosemary and White Cheddar Cheese

*(Makes 2 quarts)*

| | | | |
|---|---|---|---|
| 1 | large onion, diced | 4 oz | butter |
| 4 oz | flour | 2 qt | chicken stock |
| 1 qt | heavy cream | 6 | red bell peppers |
| 2 | rosemary sprigs | 2 C | grated white Cheddar |

Roast, peel and seed peppers, and puree in a blender or processor and set aside. Sauté onion in butter until translucent. Add flour and cook another two minutes. Add chicken stock, reduce heat and simmer about 15 minutes, until lightly thickened. Add cream, peppers and rosemary, and simmer another 15 minutes. Remove from heat, remove rosemary sprigs, and whisk in the cheese.

Bowers Harbor Inn

# Basil and Spinach Soup
With Lemon Cream

*(Makes 4 to 6 servings)*

| | | | |
|---|---|---|---|
| 1½ lb | fresh spinach | 3 T | olive oil |
| 1 | med. onion, chopped | 1 | clove garlic, pressed |
| 1 C | fresh basil leaves | 3½ C | chicken broth |
| ½ C | grated Parmesan cheese | 1 C | whipping cream |
| 2 t | lemon juice | ¼ t | grated lemon rind |
| | salt to taste | | |

Remove and discard spinach stems; rinse leaves well and drain. (Should have 16 cups, lightly packed.) In a 4-qt. kettle heat oil over medium heat, add onion and cook until soft. Mix in garlic, then add spinach and basil leaves, stirring often until leaves wilt. Add broth, bring to a boil, reduce heat, and simmer uncovered for 10 minutes. Remove spinach and basil leaves with a slotted spoon and transfer to a blender. Add a little broth and puree, then return to the pot. Mix in the cheese and ⅔ cup of the cream. Reheat to serving temperature, and salt to taste. Combine remaining cream in a medium bowl with lemon juice and zest and beat until stiff. Spoon a dollop of lemon cream on each serving of hot soup.

Cappuccino's

# Tomato-Basil-Pasta Soup

*(Makes about 4 quarts)*

| | | | |
|---|---|---|---|
| 3 C | crushed tomato | 1 | leek |
| 1 | med. onion | $^1/_2$ C | sugar |
| 1 qt | reduced chicken stock | $^1/_4$ C | dry chicken base paste |
| 4 | lg. carrots | 1 C | dried parsley |
| $^1/_2$ C | chopped fresh basil | 3 pts | heavy cream |
| $^1/_2$ lb | butter | $^1/_2$ lb | penne pasta |

Finely chop or process basil (stems and all), leeks, carrots and onion, and sauté with parsley in butter until onions are transparent. In a saucepan, add sugar to tomato and bring to boil, add stock and sautéed vegetables and bring to a simmer. Cook pasta, and combine with tomato mixture. Serve in bowls with French bread.

Cappuccino's

# Royal British Blue Stilton Cream of Vidalia Onion Soup

*(Yields about 5 quarts)*

| | | | |
|---|---|---|---|
| 6-8 C | chopped Vidalia onions | 4 C | chopped leeks |
| 4 | garlic cloves | 1 qt | chicken stock |
| $^1/_4$ C | dry chicken base paste | 1 qt | heavy cream |
| $^1/_2$ t | ground nutmeg | $^1/_8$ t | cayenne |
| 1 lb | Stilton cheese, crumbled | | |

Sauté onion, leek and garlic in butter, and puree. Make a hot-water paste with chicken base. Combine all ingredients in a large soup pot and bring nearly to a boil, until cheese melts. Watch closely to be sure it does not boil. Season to taste with additional nutmeg and Cayenne if desired. (*This may sound like a lot of onions and cheese, but owner-chef John Dozier regards this recipe much as he regards the name he gave it. The name has a lot of words, and, he says, "You can't use too many onions or too much cheese."*)

La Cuisine Amical

# Gazpacho

*(Makes 3 qts.)*

| | | | |
|---|---|---|---|
| 1¹/₂ | med. cucumber | 1 | med. green pepper |
| ¹/₄ | med. red pepper | ¹/₄ | med. yellow pepper |
| 1 C | chopped green onion | 2¹/₂ | med., fresh, ripe tomatoes |
| 2 qt | vegetable juice cocktail | ¹/₂ T | Tabasco |
| ³/₄ t | salt | ³/₄ t | fresh, cracked pepper |
| ¹/₄ C | fresh basil | | |

Wash, clean and finely dice green, red and yellow peppers. Stripe and finely dice cucumber. Seed and finely dice tomatoes. Combine half the diced vegetables in enough vegetable juice to fill a blender and process until pureed. Combine with remaining juice and vegetables, spices and herbs in a one-gallon container, stir well and chill overnight. Serve with a dollop of sour cream.

Hattie's

# Whitefish Chowder

*(Serves 12)*

| | | | |
|---|---|---|---|
| 2 T | butter | ¹/₄ C | all-purpose flour |
| 3 t | chopped garlic | ¹/₄ C | diced shallot |
| 2 C | chopped onion | 1 C | diced celery |
| ¹/₂ C | diced carrot | 1 lb | whitefish |
| 1 C | half-and-half | 3 C | clam juice |
| 1 | bay leaf | dash | cayenne pepper |
| ¹/₄ t | cumin seeds | ¹/₄ t | thyme leaf |
| ¹/₄ t | sage | dash | white pepper |
| 1¹/₂ t | dry rosemary | | |

Skin, bone and dice whitefish. Sauté garlic in butter until golden. Add shallots, onions, celery and carrots and simmer until tender. Add flour and stir. Cook three minutes on low heat. Slowly add clam juice while bringing up temperature. Add whitefish and cream and bring to a simmer. Add seasonings and simmer 30 minutes or until fish is thoroughly cooked.

Leelanau Country Inn

# Chilled Cherry Soup

*(Serves 4)*

| | | | |
|---|---|---|---|
| 100 | lg. pitted tart cherries | 2$^1$/$_2$ C | water |
| 2$^1$/$_2$ T | sugar | 5 | 2-in. cinnamon sticks |
| 1 | lemon (peel only) | 5 oz | rosé wine |
| 5 t | cornstarch | 1$^1$/$_4$ C | low-fat yogurt |
| 8 | leaves fresh mint | | |

In small saucepan, combine cherries, water, sugar, lemon peel and cinnamon sticks. Bring to a boil, reduce heat, cover and simmer 20 minutes. Strain out and discard cinnamon sticks and lemon peel. In a separate container, stir starch into wine until it dissolves, then add to cherry mixture, stirring constantly, and bring back to a boil, reduce heat, and simmer until mixture thickens. In a mixing bowl, stir 1 cup yogurt until smooth, add cherry mixture and stir to combine thoroughly. Cover and refrigerate until well chilled (overnight is best). Serve in soup cups topped with 1 T. yogurt and garnish each with a mint leaf and a cherry.

The Rowe

# Garden Sorrel Soup

| | | | | |
|---|---|---|---|---|
| 4 C | chicken broth | 2 | small carrots |
| 1 | small leek | 4 C | fresh sorrel leaves |
| 1/2 C | tiny peas | 1/2 C | butter |
| 1/2 C | flour | 1 C | cream |
| 2 C | milk | 1 T | chopped parsley |
| 1 T | snipped chives | 1/4 t | white pepper |
| | salt to taste | | |

Peel and julienne carrots. Slice leek white thinly (discard green). Wash sorrel leaves and slice thinly. Bring chicken broth to boil in medium saucepan. Add carrots and leeks and cook until tender (about 10 minutes). Meantime, in another saucepan, melt the butter, whisk in the flour, then gradually whisk in milk and cream and cook until mixture thickens. Add the chervil, chives and white pepper and, stirring constantly, add the chicken broth, carrots and leeks, then the sorrel and peas. Cook over medium-low heat for 10 minutes. Adjust seasonings and serve hot.

Roast and Toast

# Loaded Potato Soup

| | | | | |
|---|---|---|---|---|
| ¼ lb | bacon | ⅓ C | margarine |
| 1 | small onion, diced | ⅔ C | flour |
| 3 qt | chicken stock | ½ t | black pepper |
| ½ t | white pepper | 1 T | fresh, chopped parsley |
| 2 C | half-and-half | 6 | jumbo potatoes |
| 4 oz | grated Cheddar cheese | 1 C | sour cream |

Peel, cube and boil potatoes. Do not drain. Fry bacon in a stock pot until crisp. Crumble and set aside on paper towel to drain and discard most of the grease remaining in pot. Melt margarine in pot and sauté onion until soft. Add flour and mix to form a roux and cook five minutes over medium heat, stirring often. Add chicken broth, potatoes, salt, pepper and herbs. Simmer and stir until thickened. Add half-and-half (or milk) and cheese. Stir to blend. Add crumbled bacon. (*Owners Bob and Mary Keedy say this is one of the best sellers in a regular rotation of soups that make Roast and Toast a lunch-time favorite in Petoskey. Pair it with their chicken-prosciutto club sandwich for a meal hearty enough to fend off a January blizzard*).

## Sleder's

# Bean Soup

*(Makes about 6 quarts)*

| | | | |
|---|---|---|---|
| 1 lb | northern beans, soaked in hot water | 1 lb | diced carrots |
| 1 lb | diced onion | 2 lb | diced picnic ham |
| 1 T | liquid smoke | 1 oz | ham base |
| | salt and white pepper to taste | | |

Put all ingredients in a stock pot with 1 gallon of water. bring to a boil and simmer 4 hours. Season to taste. (*Ham base, in dried form similar to beef or chicken base, is available at such specialty food stores as Folgarelli's in Traverse City.*)

## Top of the Park

# Brandied Wild Mushroom Bisque

| | | | |
|---|---|---|---|
| $3/4$ oz | unsalted butter | $1/4$ C | carrots |
| $1/4$ C | celery | $1/4$ C | Spanish onions |
| 2 T | chopped dry morels | 8 oz | Portobello mushrooms |
| 2 | garlic cloves, diced | $1/2$ C | brandy |
| $1/2$ C | white wine | 1 | bay leaf |
| 1/8 t | thyme | 1 t | green peppercorns |
| 1 t | parsley | 1 C | heavy cream |
| 1 t | salt | $1/2$ t | white pepper |
| dash | cayenne pepper | 1 C | chicken stock |

Cook carrots, celery, Spanish onions, dry morel mushrooms, Portobello mushrooms and garlic in butter. Add brandy and white wine, process until smooth. Add bay leaf, thyme, heavy cream, chicken stock and spices. Heat and simmer for 30 minutes.

Spencer Creek

# Chilled Cantaloupe Soup
With Honey-Plum-Cinnamon Starburst

*(Serves 4)*

### SOUP

| | | | |
|---|---|---|---|
| 3 | ripe cantaloupes | 2 T | melon liqueur (optional) |

Quarter cantaloupes, remove meat and cut into pieces, and pulse in processor until smooth. Taste for sweetness and add melon liqueur if needed or desired. Chill in refrigerator for $2^1/_2$ hours.

### PLUM SAUCE

| | | | |
|---|---|---|---|
| 6 | ripe plums | 2 T | honey |
| 1 C | Riesling wine | 2 T | sugar |
| 1 | cinnamon stick | 1 T | lemon juice |

Pit and quarter plums and combine with remaining ingredients in sauce pot, and cook down on medium heat until sauce starts to thicken (about $^1/_2$ hour). Strain and refrigerate.

### PRESENTATION

Place cantaloupe soup in bowls and spoon two dollops of plum sauce into each bowl. With a knife, shape plum-sauce dollops into stars. Garnish with julienne of mint.

Tapawingo

# Grilled Corn Soup
## With Roasted Pepper Cream

*(Serves 4-6)*

ROASTED PEPPER CREAM

| | | | |
|---|---|---|---|
| 2 | red bell peppers | 4 T | sour cream |
| | salt, pepper to taste | | |

Roast peppers over grill or flame until skins blacken. Cool in damp towel 5 minutes then remove skin, seeds and veins. Process remainder in blender until smooth. Add sour cream, salt and pepper.

GRILLED CORN SOUP

| | | | |
|---|---|---|---|
| 6 | ears corn in husk | 1/2 C | chopped carrot |
| 2 T | olive oil | 1 | seeded, minced jalapeño |
| 1/4 C | chopped celery | 1/2 C | chopped onion |
| 4 C | chicken stock | 2 | cloves roasted garlic |
| 1 C | heavy cream | | cumin, salt, cayenne to taste |

Grill corn 10 minutes over low fire; then husk and cut kernels from ear. Sweat celery, carrots, onion, garlic and pepper in oil in large saucepan until transparent. Add chicken stock. Bring to boil, then reduce heat and simmer 5 minutes. Add corn kernels and simmer 10 more minutes. Place all ingredients in a blender and process about 2 minutes. Strain through a sieve into another saucepan, add cream, cook over low heat 5 minutes. Season to taste, then drizzle decoratively with roasted pepper cream. (*Tapawingo sometimes uses a cilantro cream instead of the roasted pepper cream; this is a sieved puree of cilantro and parsley mixed with a little sour cream.*)

Walloon Lake Inn

# Pear-Pea-Watercress Soup

*(Serves 10)*

| | | | |
|---|---|---|---|
| 1 | onion, peeled & sliced | 1 | pear, peeled, cored, sliced |
| ¹/₄ C | butter | 10 oz | peas |
| 4 C | chicken broth | ¹/₄ C | sherry |
| ¹/₄ t | dried thyme | 1 | bunch watercress |

Cook onion and pear in butter until soft. Add peas, broth, sherry, thyme. Simmer 8 minutes, add watercress, and simmer 3 more minutes. Serve hot or cold.

Windows

# Morel and Zucchini Bisque

| | | | |
|---|---|---|---|
| 2 | potatoes, peeled and diced | 1 | onion, peeled and diced |
| 2 | shallots, peeled and diced | 1 T | butter |
| 1 T | olive oil | 3 | zucchinis, diced |
| ¹/₄ lb | morels, diced | 3 C | milk |
| 2 C | whole cream | 1 C | sherry |
| ¹/₄ lb | morels, quartered as garnish | | |

Slowly sauté onions, potatoes, and shallots in butter and olive oil until light golden brown. Add diced zucchini and morels, simmer for 10 minutes. Add cream and milk, simmer until potatoes are soft. Puree soup. Add sherry, season with salt and pepper, garnish with quartered morels. Thin with milk if desired.

Reflections

# Smoked Shrimp Chowder

*(Serves 8)*

| | | | | |
|---|---|---|---|---|
| 1/2 lb | smoked shrimp | 1/2 C | minced red onion |
| 1 oz | butter | 1 qt | chicken stock |
| 1 | small bay leaf | 1/2 C | white rice |
| 1/2 C | diced red bell pepper | 2 C | frozen corn |
| 3 C | heavy cream | 1 t | fresh thyme |
| | salt, pepper to taste | | |

Sweat the onion in butter. Add chicken stock, bay leaf and rice, and simmer 20 minutes. Add shrimp, diced pepper and corn, and simmer 20 minutes more. Finish with cream and seasonings before serving.

Stafford's Bay View Inn

# Great Lakes Chowder

*(Makes 1 gallon)*

| | | | | |
|---|---|---|---|---|
| 1 1/4 lb | walleye | 1/2 lb | whitefish |
| 1/4 lb | smoked whitefish | 2 1/2 oz | leeks, sliced thin |
| 1/4 lb | onion, diced medium | 2 1/2 oz | smoked bacon, diced |
| 1/4 lb | butter | 5 C | cream |
| 1 1/2 lb | potato, diced & cooked | 1 oz | clam base |
| 1 | bay leaf | | |
| | salt, thyme, white pepper, coriander, Old Bay to taste | | |

Skin, debone and dice fish. Boil in 1/2 gallon of water. When done, strain out fish and let cool. Add cream to liquid and return fish to pot. Fry bacon in skillet. Add butter, leek and onion, cook until transparent, and combine with stock mixture. Thicken as desired with flour. Add potatoes, season, and simmer until thoroughly heated.

# Rose Room, Stafford's Perry Hotel

# Onion Soup

*(Makes about 1 gallon)*

| | | | |
|---|---|---|---|
| 1 oz | olive oil | $1/4$ | onion, chopped |
| 1 | celery stalk, chopped | $1/2$ | carrot, chopped |
| $1/2$ oz | tomato paste | 1 | sprig rosemary |
| 1 t | crushed black pepper | 5 oz | pale, dry sherry |
| 4 C | chicken stock | 4 C | beef stock |
| 6 C | sweet onion, sliced | $1/2$ oz | garlic paste |
| 1 oz | Cognac | | seasoned croutons |
| | sliced mild cheese | | |

Heat oil in sauté pan and brown chopped onion, celery and carrot. Add tomato paste, bring to simmer, add rosemary, pepper, sherry and stocks and simmer 1 hour. Strain and reserve. Brown sliced onions in heavy-bottom pan until golden. Deglaze with Cognac. Combine with stock and simmer 15 minutes. Adjust seasoning. To serve, ladle into cups, sprinkle on croutons, top with cheese, and place under broiler until bubbly on top.

# Weathervane

# Potato-Leek Soup

*(Makes about 2 quarts)*

| | | | |
|---|---|---|---|
| 3 | lg. potatoes | $1/2$ C | diced leek |
| $1/2$ C | diced Spanish onion | 4 C | chicken stock |
| | salt, pepper, heavy cream to taste | | chives for garnish |

Peel and dice potatoes. Bring stock to boil, add potatoes, and cook about halfway, then add leek and onion. Cook thoroughly so potatoes fall apart. Puree mixture in blender or processor. Return to stove over low heat, add cream to lighten and thin as desired. Season to taste. Serve garnished with chopped or whole chive.

# Duck and Sausage Gumbo

*(Makes approx. 4 qts.)*

STOCK

| | | | |
|---|---|---|---|
| 1 | whole duck | 2 | carrots |
| 1 | onion (skin on) | 3 | celery stalks |
| 1 | garlic bulb, halved | 3 | bay leaves |
| 2C | tomato puree | | thyme |

Roast duck until crispy and let cool. Remove meat. Reserve fat. In 2-quart saucepan, combine duck bones and all remaining ingredients. Fill with water. Simmer 6 hours. Strain and reserve.

SOUP

| | | | |
|---|---|---|---|
| 2 lb | sausage (andouille or kielbasa) | 4 | green bell peppers |
| 4 | onions | 3 C | okra, sliced |
| 2 T | chopped garlic | | cayenne pepper or Cajun spice |

Cut sausage into half-inch slices and bake to render off any grease. Set aside. Cut peppers and onions into $^3/_4$-inch squares. In a sauce pot make a roux of about $1^1/_2$ C of reserved duck fat and an equal amount of flour, cooked slowly until dark brown in color (about 20-30 minutes). Add onion and peppers, chopped garlic and cayenne and continue cooking, stirring, for 10 minutes. Add strained duck stock and simmer 20 minutes. Add cooked sausage, chopped duck meat and okra. Season to taste.

# Uncle Jimmy's Vegetable Soup

*(Makes about 12 servings)*

| | | | | |
|---|---|---|---|---|
| 1 lb | stew beef | 1 T | olive oil |
| 2 | med. onions, diced | 1 pt | beef stock or broth |
| 2 | carrots, diced | 4 | celery stalks, sliced thin |
| 2 | med. white potatoes, diced | 3 C | peeled, chopped tomatoes |
| 1 C | chopped fresh parsley | 2 | bay leaves |
| $^1/_2$ t | thyme | 6 drops | cider vinegar |
| pinch | cinnamon | | salt, pepper to taste |

Trim beef of fat and dice into $^1/_2$-inch pieces. Brown in stock pot with oil over high heat, with half the chopped onion. Add stock or broth, $1^1/_2$ quarts of water, bay leaf and seasonings. Bring to boiling, reduce heat and simmer rapidly for 90 minutes. Meantime chop or dice all vegetables and combine in a bowl with juice from tomatoes and just enough water to cover so potatoes won't brown. After stock has simmered 90 minutes, stir in all the vegetables and juice, add parsley (and up to a pint of water, if more volume is desired). Return to boiling and simmer gently another 90 minutes or until soup no longer has "watery" taste. If desired add a splash of red wine before serving. *(Graydon's Dad, whom everyone called "Uncle Jimmy," was no serious cook, but he grilled steak once a week, made no-nonsense salad dressing—salt, pepper, oil and vinegar—and sometimes fixed Welsh rarebit. In mid-life, for some reason, he also took to making this vegetable soup. We still make three or four big batches a year. It keeps for days in the fridge and freezes well.)*

# Salads

American Spoon Foods

## Curried Rice Luncheon Salad

*(Serves 4)*

| | | | |
|---|---|---|---|
| 2 C | cooked white basmati rice | $^1/_2$ | skinless, boneless chicken breast |
| $^1/_2$ C | pineapple chunks | 2 T | diced red pepper |
| 2 T | diced green pepper | 2 T | diced onion |
| 2 T | toasted almond slivers | 2 T | dried tart cherries |
| $^1/_2$ C | Flurry of Curry relish * | 1 T | peanut oil |
| 1 T | chopped cilantro | 1 t | finely minced garlic |
| | salt, pepper to taste | | |

Heat peanut oil in a large saute pan. Add chicken and saute over high heat, stirring constantly, for one minute. Add peppers, onion, garlic and pineapple and continue sauteing until pineapple is slightly browned and chicken is thoroughly cooked. Remove from heat and add remaining ingredients. Stir or toss to mix well and serve immediately for a warm salad or chill to serve later as a cold salad. *(This recipe is from Chris Chickering, research-and-development chef at American Spoon Foods, who sometimes makes a vegetarian dish of it by omitting chicken, and sometimes uses brown or white rice instead of basmati.)*

*an American Spoon Foods product

American Spoon Foods

# Warm Chicken Pasta Salad

*(Serves 4)*

| | | | | |
|---|---|---|---|---|
| 2 T | olive oil | 2 | boneless, skinless breasts |
| $^1/_2$ lb | fusilli, cooked al dente | 1$^1/_2$ t | minced garlic |
| 16 pcs | asparagus | $^1/_2$ | sweet red pepper, julienne |
| $^1/_3$ C | Tangy Ginger Dazzler * | 1 T | chopped fresh parsley |
| 1 T | chopped fresh cilantro | | salt and pepper to taste |

Trim fat and cut chicken into thin slices. Peel and trim asparagus. Discard 1-2 inches of butt ends and cut tips into 2-inch pieces. Cook one minute in rapidly boiling water, drain and refresh with ice water. When completely chilled, drain again. Bring oil to high heat in a large, non-stick pan. Season chicken strips with salt and pepper and saute, stirring, for 2 minutes. Add garlic, asparagus, red pepper strips and cooked pasta and continue cooking another minute. Add Tangy Ginger Dazzler and stir. Add chopped parsley and cilantro, and serve. *(This recipe is from Larry Forgione, owner of An American Place in New York as well as co-founder and co-owner of American Spoon Foods and creator of many of its recipes.)*

*an American Spoon Foods product

La Bécasse

# Chèvre and Dried Cherry Salad

*(Serves 6)*

| | | | | |
|---|---|---|---|---|
| $^2/_3$ C | extra-virgin olive oil | | $^1/_3$ C | white-wine tarragon vinegar |
| 1 T | minced fresh tarragon (or 1t dried) | | $^1/_2$ | red bell pepper, finely diced |
| 1 t | Dijon mustard | | 1 t | lemon juice |
| $^1/_2$ t | salt | | 6-8 | twists of fresh black pepper |
| $^1/_2$ lb | spinach | | $^1/_2$ | head of romaine |
| 6 oz | crumbled chèvre | | $^3/_4$ C | dried cherries |
| $^3/_4$ C | toasted sliced almonds | | $^1/_2$ | red onion, finely sliced |
| 1 t | red bell pepper, finely chopped | | | |

Wash and dry spinach and romaine, and tear into bite-size pieces. For dressing, whisk together oil, vinegar, tarragon, diced bell pepper, mustard, lemon juice, salt, and pepper (makes about 1 cup). Toss salad with about half the vinaigrette. Arrange greens on six plates and sprinkle each with chèvre, cherries, almonds, red onion and chopped bell pepper. Drizzle with additional vinaigrette.

Arboretum

# Warm Tomato Salad
With Gorgonzola Vinaigrette

*(Serves 4)*

| | | | | |
|---|---|---|---|---|
| $^1/_2$ lb | bacon | | $^1/_4$ C | balsamic vinegar |
| $^1/_2$ C | crumbled Gorgonzola | | 4 | large tomatoes |
| $^1/_4$ C | toasted pine nuts | | | |

Cook bacon until crisp, drain well and dice, and set aside. Heat vinegar over low heat, and when hot, whisk in Gorgonzola, and set aside. Thinly slice tomatoes and arrange one on each plate. Warm in oven 2-4 minutes. Evenly distribute the Gorgonzola vinaigrette over the tomato slices and garnish with diced bacon and toasted nuts.

## The Bluebird

# Thai Salad

*(Serves 8-10)*

| | | | |
|---|---|---|---|
| 1 C | white vinegar | 1 1/2 t | minced fresh ginger |
| 1 C | sugar | 1 t | lime zest |
| 1 C | water | 1 C | fresh basil, mint, cilantro |
| 1/2 t | hot sauce (e.g., Siracha) | 1 t | salt |
| 2 t | finely minced garlic | | |

assorted vegetables (e.g., sprouts, tomato, red onion, carrot, cucumber, peanuts, sunflower seeds, celery), sliced or julienne

assorted greens torn in large pieces

Mix dressing ingredients a day ahead if possible. Make up salads topped with vegetables. Splash on the dressing just before serving. Sprinkle liberally with herbs and garnish with nuts or seeds. (*Chef Cris Telgard says this salad is also "great" topped with slices of grilled chicken breast, grilled shrimp, or thinly sliced grilled steak.*)

## Chef Charles

# Mediterranean Salad

*(Serves 2)*

| | | | |
|---|---|---|---|
| 5 C | bite-size pieces of washed romaine | 8 | artichoke heart quarters |
| 8 | Sicilian olives | 8 | slices green and red bell pepper |
| 4 T | crumbled feta | 20 | thinly sliced red onion rings |
| 2 T | shredded Parmesan | 6-8 | slices Roma tomato |

Combine all ingredients and toss with your favorite vinaigrette. (*Frankly, we'd simply season 1t. of vinegar with salt and whisk it with 1 T. of garlic-infused oil.*)

Left Bank

# Simple Caesar Salad

*(Dressing recipe yields about 1 quart)*

## DRESSING

| | | | |
|---|---|---|---|
| 16 | garlic cloves | $^3/_4$ T | Dijon mustard |
| 2 t | kosher salt | 2 T | white wine vinegar |
| 2 t | cracked pepper | $^3/_4$ C | lemon juice |
| 1 C | grated Parmesan | 2 oz | anchovy |
| $2^2/_3$ C | olive oil | | |

## SALAD

romaine Lettuce                     garlic-parsley croutons

Combine all dressing ingredients except salt, pepper and oil and process until well blended—one or two minutes. With machine still running, add oil in a slow, steady stream. Add salt and pepper to taste. Continue processing until mixture is emulsified. Pour over romaine leaves and garnish with garlic-parsley croutons.

Monte Bianco

# Insalata Cesar

*(Serves 4)*

| | | | | |
|---|---|---|---|---|
| 1 | egg yolk | 1 t | Dijon mustard |
| 2 T | red wine vinegar | 2 | chopped anchovies |
| 1 T | freshly squeezed lemon juice | 1 T | freshly chopped garlic |
| ¹/₂ t | Worcestershire sauce | 1 C | olive oil |
| 1 | lemon | 2 | med. heads of romaine lettuce |
| 3 | handfuls of croutons | 6 T | freshly grated Parmesan cheese |
| | salt, coarse black pepper to taste | | |

Wash lettuce, discarding outer leaves. Cut into pieces about one inch square. Wrap in paper towels and chill well for at least one hour. Bring all dressing ingredients to room temperature. Combine vinegar, mustard, anchovies, lemon juice, garlic and Worcestershire in a blender or food processor and mix at high speed until the mixture starts to thicken. Then very gradually drizzle olive oil into mixture while continuing to process. Season to taste with pepper and salt. Thin if desired with additional fresh lemon juice. Add extra garlic and anchovies to taste, if desired. Dress salad in large bowl and add croutons and Parmesan (*Monte Bianco's Mary Kelly thinks "Reggiano" Parmesan is best*). Toss thoroughly and serve immediately on chilled salad plates, adding extra freshly ground black pepper if desired.

## Old Mission Tavern

# Raspberry Vinaigrette Salad

*(Serves 2)*

| | | | | |
|---|---|---|---|---|
| $3/4$ C | walnut oil | | $1/4$ C | raspberry vinegar |
| $1/4$ C | raspberry | | 1 | clove garlic |
| 1 | green onion (top and white) | | 1 head | Bibb lettuce |
| $1/2$ | med onion sliced thin | | $1/4$ C | dried cherries |
| $1/4$ C | toasted walnuts | | | |

Chop onion and garlic and add vinegar and raspberry, and puree in food processor, pulsing on and off. Drizzling walnut oil into mixture, continue processing until dressing is creamy. Toss a salad of Bibb lettuce, thinly sliced onions, dried cherries and toasted walnuts, and dress.


## Rose Room, Perry Hotel

# Cherry Vinaigrette Salad

*(Makes 1 pint of dressing)*

| | | | | |
|---|---|---|---|---|
| $3/4$ C | oil | | $1/2$ C | heavy cream |
| $1/4$ C | raspberry vinegar | | $1/4$ C | sugar |
| $1/4$ C | sweet dark cherries, pitted | | | black pepper |
| | green onion | | | assorted fresh fruit, nuts |
| | assorted light greens, such as Bibb or Boston lettuce | | | |

Puree cherries. Whip sugar and vinegar until sugar dissolves. Add cream and whip until mixture starts to thicken. While continuing to whip, slowly drizzle in the oil until fully incorporated. Add fruit. Arrange the greens, top with fruit, nuts and sliced green onion. Dress, and add freshly ground pepper.

# On the Edge

# Caesar Salad
### With Grilled, Herb-marinated Chicken

*(Serves 8)*

### GRILLED CHICKEN

| | | | | |
|---|---|---|---|---|
| 4 | skinless, boneless breasts | | 1 T | fresh oregano |
| 1 T | fresh thyme | | 1 T | fresh rosemary |
| 4 | garlic cloves, crushed | | 1 T | fresh Italian parsley |
| 1/4 C | olive oil | | | |

Mix all ingredients thoroughly, and marinate chicken breasts in a bowl overnight. Remove from marinade and grill.

### SALAD

| | | | | |
|---|---|---|---|---|
| 3 | garlic cloves | | 1 t | salt |
| 3 | anchovies | | 4 | capers |
| 3/4 C | olive oil | | 2 T | lemon juice |
| 1/2 C | grated Parmesan | | 1 | egg |
| 2 T | Worcestershire sauce | | 2 t | black pepper |
| 1 t | dry mustard | | 1/2 t | Tabasco |
| 2 | heads romaine lettuce | | | |

Mash garlic, anchovies, salt and capers in 1/4 cup of oil to make a paste. Place in blender with eggs. Thoroughly mix mustard, pepper, lemon juice, Tabasco and Worcestershire, add to blender and mix thoroughly while slowly and steadily adding remaining oil in a continuous stream. Toss romaine in a large bowl with the dressing, add chicken, arrange salad on plates, and sprinkle liberally with Parmesan cheese.

Spencer Creek

# Baby Spinach Salad
With Cambozola, Pecan and Phyllo Crouton and Sour Cherry Vinaigrette

*(Serves 6-8)*

## VINAIGRETTE

| | | | | |
|---|---|---|---|---|
| 1 C | dried sour cherries | | 3 T | red wine vinegar |
| 1 T | honey | | $1/4$ C | olive oil |
| 1 T | fresh lime juice | | 1 t | kosher salt |
| 1 t | white pepper | | | |

This is best made a day in advance. Reconstitute cherries. Place $1/2$ cup cherries in food processor with vinegar, honey, lime juice, salt, and white pepper. Pulse until cherries are chopped fine. Slowly add oil until mixture is well combined. Remove from processor and add remaining cherries. Leave overnight at room temperature.

## CROUTONS

| | | | | |
|---|---|---|---|---|
| 6 oz | cambozola with paper off | | $1/4$ C | toasted pecan |
| 4 | sheets phyllo | | 4 T | honey |
| 1 T | hot water | | | |

Combine honey and water, lay down 1 sheet of phyllo and brush with honey mixture and repeat with remaining phyllo. Cut into diamond shapes, place on parchment paper and bake at 400°F until golden brown (8-12 minutes ). Let cool. Crush pecans very fine and fold into cambozola. Spread onto phyllo croutons.

## SALAD

| | | | | |
|---|---|---|---|---|
| 8 C | baby spinach | | $3/4$ C | toasted pecan |
| $1/2$ | red onion, julienne | | 1 C | dried cherries |
| | fresh chives for garnish | | | |

Toss spinach and pecans in large salad bowl with 6 ounces vinaigrette. Place on individual plates and top with onion. Place 3 phyllo croutons around salad. Garnish with chives and dried cherries.

## Stafford's Pier

# Goat Cheese Salad

*(Serves 8)*

| | | | | |
|---|---|---|---|---|
| 9 oz | olive oil | | 3 oz | balsamic vinegar |
| 1 T | Dijon mustard | | 3 T | mango chutney |
| 1 lb | Bibb, radicchio | | 2 | lg. tomatoes, quartered |
| 1 | lg. leek, sliced | | 1/2 lb | feta cheese |
| 4 | strips bacon, cooked, crumbled | | 4 T | sesame seed |
| | black pepper to taste | | | |

Wash and dry lettuces. Make dressing by pureeing chutney in blender, adding oil, vinegar and mustard and blending until smooth. Build salads by arranging Bibb and radicchio on plates and garnishing with bacon, tomato, feta and leek. Sprinkle with sesame and pepper, and spoon on dressing.

## Stafford's Pier

# Spinach-Cashew Salad

| | | | | |
|---|---|---|---|---|
| 1/2 C | hot water | | 3/4 C | honey |
| 1/4 C | lemon juice | | 1/4 C | white-wine vinegar |
| 1 T | chopped dill weed | | 1 T | soy sauce |
| 1 T | garlic paste | | 1 1/2 C | salad oil |
| | fresh spinach leaves | | | mandarin oranges |
| | shallots, diced | | | enoki mushrooms |
| | cashews | | | |

Wash, drain and dry spinach leaves. Mix all dressing ingredients thoroughly in a bowl with a wire whisk. (Be sure water is hot.) Continuing to whip, slowly add oil until fully incorporated. Drizzle over greens. (This will make about 3 cups of dressing; refrigerate any unused portion.) Garnish with orange, shallots, mushrooms and cashews.

Reflections

# Monterey Chicken Salad

*(Serves 6)*

| | | | | |
|---|---|---|---|---|
| 3 C | chopped cooked chicken breast | | 3 | Granny Smith apples |
| 1 T | lemon juice | | 1 C | sour cream |
| 1 C | mayonnaise | | 1 C | diced celery |
| 1 C | cashews | | | salt, pepper to taste |
| | assorted fresh fruit | | | |

Core and dice apples, coat with lemon juice to prevent browning, then mix thoroughly with other ingredients. Serve surrounded with fresh fruit (e.g., kiwi, pineapple, berries, melon). Garnish with cashews.

The Authors

# Eden Salad
## With Toasted Almonds

*(Serves 4)*

| | | | | |
|---|---|---|---|---|
| 2 | med. tart apples | | 1 oz | raspberry vinegar |
| 2 oz | olive oil | | 6 | green onions, chopped |
| ¹/₂ C | sliced, roasted almonds | | | assorted greens |
| | salt, pepper to taste | | | |

Core apples and finely chop or dice. Marinate in a thoroughly mixed dressing of vinegar, oil, salt, pepper, and onion. Serve over salad greens on individual plates, and top each salad with sliced almonds.

# The Authors

# Grapefruit Salad
With Fennel and Parmesan

*(Serves 4-6)*

| | | | | |
|---|---|---|---|---|
| | various mixed, fresh greens | | 4 | spring onions (whites), sliced thin |
| 1 | grapefruit | | 1 | mashed garlic clove |
| $^1/_4$ t | salt | | 3 T | white-wine vinegar |
| 1 t | Dijon mustard | | $^1/_2$ C | olive oil |
| $^1/_3$ C | minced parsley | | 1 t | fennel (or anise) seed |
| 2 T | grated Parmesan | | | |

Wash and dry greens and put in salad bowl. Sprinkle with onion. Section grapefruit, reserving 3 T. of juice and adding sections to salad (cut in half if they're large). Thoroughly mix dressing of garlic, grapefruit juice, vinegar, mustard, parsley and oil. Dress salad. Sprinkle with fennel and Parmesan. Toss well and serve.

# The Authors

# Summer Citrus Salad
With Lime and Ginger Dressing

*(Serves 4)*

| | | | | |
|---|---|---|---|---|
| | assorted summer greens | | 1 | orange |
| 4 | green onions (whites only) | | 2 T | toasted sliced almonds |
| 1 | lime (juice only) | | 2 | crushed garlic cloves |
| 4 T | olive oil | | $^1/_8$ t | powdered ginger |
| | salt to taste | | | |

Wash and dry greens and arrange on plates. Peel and section orange and apportion pieces on greens. Thinly slice onion and sprinkle on salads along with almonds. Thoroughly mix remaining ingredients to make dressing and sprinkle evenly on plates.

# Char-Grilled Sirloin Salad
## With Horseradish Chutney Salsa

*(Serves 4)*

| | | | | |
|---|---|---|---|---|
| 1 lb | sirloin steak, trimmed | | 8 | med. redskin potatoes |
| 1 T | olive oil | | 2 T | chopped fresh parsley |
| 2 | garlic cloves, crushed | | 4 T | Major Grey's chutney |
| 1 t | fresh horseradish | | 2 T | salsa |
| ¹/₂ t | Dijon mustard | | 2 t | mayonnaise |
| 2 | medium tomatoes | | | assorted fresh salad greens |
| | salt, black pepper to taste | | | |

Rub beef with salt and pepper. Quarter potatoes and toss with oil, parsley and garlic in a baking dish and roast until done (about 40 minutes at 375ºF), and set aside. Make dressing of chutney, mayonnaise, mustard, horseradish, and salsa (commercial salsa is suitable). Arrange greens on plates and garnish with sliced tomato. Char-grill steak and potatoes. Let beef rest 5 minutes, then slice in strips, arrange on greens and surround with potato. Drizzle on beef juices. Spoon dressing on top.

# Fish and Seafood

Andante

# Whitefish in Potato Crust
With Dilled Gewurztraminer Butter Sauce

*(Serves 4)*

### WHITEFISH IN POTATO CRUST

| | | | |
|---|---|---|---|
| 2 | 16-oz. whitefish filets | 4 | large baking potatoes |
| 2 | shallots | 2 T | clarified butter |
| | salt, white pepper to taste | | |

Skin and pin-bone filets and cut in half. Peel potatoes and shallots and shred with a hand grater or food processor. Blanch quickly in boiling water and drain. Rinse with cold water, press out as much moisture as possible, and season with salt and white pepper. On a flat surface, form four thin layers of potato mixture the same size as each of the four pieces of fish. Press potato mixture gently into fish. Gently lift with a large spatula and sauté in clarified butter until golden. Turn very carefully and brown bottom an equal time.

### GEWURZTRAMINER BUTTER

| | | | |
|---|---|---|---|
| 2 C | Gewurztraminer | 1/4 C | shallots, finely chopped |
| 1/2 C | cream | 6 oz | unsalted butter |
| 1/4 C | fresh dill | | salt, cayenne pepper to taste |

Cut butter into half-inch cubes. In a saucepan, reduce wine and shallots by half. Add cream and cook until again reduce by half or thickened. Add butter and stir in, bit by bit, until melted. Do not allow to boil. Season to taste, and serve.

## Stafford's Bay View Inn

# Baked Scallops
With Shrimp Garnish

| | | | |
|---|---|---|---|
| 1 lb | fresh scallops | 8 | shrimp, cooked |
| 1 C | crushed croutons | 2 oz | shredded Muenster |
| 2 oz | shredded Cheddar | 2 T | lemon juice |
| 2 t | garlic powder | 2 T | butter |
| 1/4 C | green onion, diced | 1 t | sherry |
| | salt and white pepper to taste | | |

Peel, devein and cook shrimp and set aside. Combine all remaining ingredients in bowl and apportion among individual buttered baking boats or ramekins. Bake at 350F about 10 minutes. Garnish with shrimp and brown under broiler before serving.

## The Bluebird

# Grilled Marlin
With Barbecue Butter

*(Serves 6)*

| | | | |
|---|---|---|---|
| 6 | 8-oz. swordfish steaks | 1 t | minced fresh garlic |
| 2 T | yellow mustard | 1/4 C | soy sauce |
| 1/2 lb | butter | 2 t | ketchup |
| 1 T | Worcestershire | dash | Tabasco |

Combine all ingredients except fish in a saucepan and simmer 15 minutes. Brush fish and grill top with vegetable oil. Grill fish 2/3 through and brush with sauce, then turn. Brush grilled side liberally with sauce and finish. When just done, brush again with sauce. Serve garnished with parsley or sliced scallion. (*This barbecue butter is a delicious accent to any grilled fish. The Bluebird serves it on swordfish, marlin, and salmon. The barbecue butter is rather salty and you may want to adjust the amount of soy sauce.*)

## Elk River Inn

# Whitefish Parmigiana

*(Per serving)*

| | | | |
|---|---|---|---|
| 1 | pinboned whitefish filet | 1/4 C | finely diced onion |
| 2 T | dried Italian seasonings | 1 T | grated Parmesan cheese |
| 1 1/2 C | ranch-style dressing (e.g., Hidden Valley) | | |

Mix onion, dressing and seasonings thoroughly and spread on filet (it will be fairly thick). Top with Parmesan. Bake on lightly buttered baking sheet 12-15 minutes at 400F until golden brown. If necessary, finish under broiler for 20-30 seconds.

## Poppycock's

# Grilled Salmon
### With Mushroom-Leek Ragout

*(Serves 4)*

Salmon

| | | | |
|---|---|---|---|
| 4 | 6-oz. salmon filets | 1 T | vegetable oil |
| | salt, pepper to taste | | |

Lightly oil filets, season with salt and pepper, and char-grill.

Ragout

| | | | |
|---|---|---|---|
| 3 | julienned leek whites | 2 C | cream |
| 1 t | minced garlic | 2 oz | sweet vermouth |
| 2 C | sliced mushrooms | | salt, pepper to taste |

Heat leeks and mushrooms in a pot until they steam. Add garlic, vermouth, cream and simmer until cream thickens and vegetables are cooked (about 12 minutes). Season with salt and pepper. Keep warm, and spoon over grilled salmon.

Hattie's

# Sautéed Whitefish
With Orange-Ginger Relish

*(Serves 10)*

## ORANGE GINGER RELISH

| | | | |
|---|---|---|---|
| 2/3 | med. onion | 2 1/2 T | chopped fresh ginger |
| 1 | med. orange | 2 T | froz. orange juice concentrate |
| 2 1/2 T | dry white wine | 1 t | white wine vinegar |
| 4 t | honey | 1/3 C | butter, softened |
| dash | white pepper | 1/3 t | salt |

Peel and chop ginger, onions and oranges and combine in heavy saucepan with frozen juice concentrate, wine, vinegar and honey. Simmer until all ingredients are tender. Drain some liquid and puree remainder in processor. Let cool to about 110°F. Add softened butter while continuing to mix in processor and blend to bright yellow paste. Season and taste.

## SAUTÉED WHITEFISH

| | | | |
|---|---|---|---|
| 10 | whitefish filets | 4 T | Dijon mustard |
| 3/4 C | flour | 3/4 C | sesame seeds |
| 4 T | butter or oil | | |

Mix flour and sesame seeds. Brush flesh side of filets with mustard, dip in flour-seed mixture and shake off excess. Sauté in butter or oil, turning once. Serve garnished with relish.

Leelanau Country Inn

# Pan Fried Perch
With Lemon-butter Sauce

*(Serves 4)*

### LEMON BUTTER SAUCE

$^1/_3$ C  lemon juice                    $^1/_4$ lb  butter

Cut butter into half-inch cubes. Bring lemon juice to a boil and remove from heat. Feed butter cubes into juice one at a time, stirring vigorously until melted. You can use a hand-held mixture at high speed; it's impossible to stir this mixture too much. (This can be made in advance in larger quantities, and can be stored in freezer up to six months).

### PAN FRIED PERCH

| | | | |
|---|---|---|---|
| 24 | perch filets | 2 C | milk |
| $^1/_2$ t | paprika | $^1/_4$ C | butter |
| $^1/_4$ C | dry sherry | $^1/_2$ C | flour |
| $^1/_4$ C | lemon juice | 2 T | chopped fresh parsley |

Thoroughly scale and debone filets. In a sealable container, layer filets with milk, making sure all filets are thoroughly covered. Seal container and refrigerate 24 hours (or up to 3 days). Drain and discard milk, leaving filets moist. In sauté pan, melt $^1/_2$ stick butter until very hot (but not brown). Lightly dredge moist filets in flour and place in sauté pan, skin side up. Quickly add sherry to pan around, but not over, filets. Cook until golden brown, turning once to brown on both sides. After arranging on plates, top with hot lemon-butter sauce and sprinkle with parsley.

## Leelanau Country Inn

# Swordfish Piccata

*(Serves 4)*

| | | | |
|---|---|---|---|
| 4 | 6-oz. swordfish steaks | 1/4 C | flour |
| 1/2 C | butter | 1 T | capers |
| 2 | lemons, quartered | 1/8 t. | salt |
| 1/8 t | black pepper | 2 T | chopped fresh parsley |

Sprinkle steaks with salt and pepper and let sit 5 minutes. Dredge steaks in flour and shake off excess. In sauté pan, melt half the butter and heat until foaming but not browning. Brown steaks in pan 2 minutes on each side. In separate sauté pan, melt remaining butter and heat until foaming but not browning. Add capers and lemon wedges, squeezing the juice into the pan first. Cook 3 minutes, remove and discard lemon rind and any seeds. Place fish into serving dish or plates, top with caper-butter sauce, sprinkle with parsley. (*The Leelanau Country Inn's Linda and John Sisson, who have fresh fish flown in daily, include this recipe in their own* Leelanau Country Inn Cookery *book, in which they say any fish recipe depends on good, fresh fish. They suggest that if you can't find fresh swordfish, then other fish can be substituted, such as salmon, whitefish, perch or even mako shark.*)

One Water Street

# Poached Salmon
With Pecan Lime Butter

*(Serves 4-6)*

LIME BUTTER

| | | | | |
|---|---|---|---|---|
| 1 lb | butter | 1 | | lime |
| 1 | shallot, minced | 1 C | | chopped pecans |
| 1 T | Worcestershire | | | salt, pepper to taste |

Soften butter at room temperature. Add zest and juice of entire lime and all remaining ingredients. Combine by hand, roll into logs using waxed paper, and refrigerate for at least 2 hours. (*This will make more than you need; refrigerate unused portion*).

SALMON

| | | | |
|---|---|---|---|
| 2 lb | fresh salmon, skinned and boned | 1 C | white wine |
| 2 T | capers | 2 | shallots, diced |

Remove enough lime butter from refrigerator to sauce salmon. Add wine, shallots, capers to about 2 quarts water in a large pan, bring to a boil and reduce heat, and poach salmon until firm to the touch. Plate salmon and top with lime butter.

Rose Room, Stafford's Perry Hotel

# Shrimp Champagne

*(Serves 6)*

| | | | |
|---|---|---|---|
| 6 oz | olive oil | 28-30 | lg. shrimp |
| 1 | sm. green bell pepper, julienned | 1 | sm. red bell pepper, julienned |
| 1 | sm. yellow bell pepper, julienned | 1 | lg. tomato, chopped |
| 2C | sliced mushrooms | 1 C | champagne |
| 2 C | whipping cream | | basil, garlic, salt, pepper to taste |

Peel, wash and devein shrimp and sauté in oil in large pan 1 minute on high heat. Add peppers and mushrooms and continue sautéing another 1-2 minutes. Add tomato, champagne, cream and seasonings, and simmer until sauce thickens. Serve over pasta.

Spencer Creek

# Seared Salmon Filet
With Scallop, Lemon and Hazelnut Sauce on Wilted Spinach and Wild Rice Cake

(*Serves 4*)

### WILD RICE CAKES AND SPINACH

| | | | | |
|---|---|---|---|---|
| 1 C | cooked wild rice | | 1 t | vegetable oil |
| 3 T | shallots, diced | | 1 | egg |
| 1/2 C | half-and-half | | 2 T | flour |
| 1/4 t | cayenne pepper | | 1 T | dried chives |
| 4 C | packed spinach | | 2 t | butter |
| | salt and freshly ground black pepper to taste | | | |

In medium bowl whip egg and half-and-half. Add wild rice, shallots, flour, chives, cayenne. Add salt and pepper. Fold together. Bring small sauté pan to medium heat, add oil, ladle in 3 ounces of batter per rice cake, and cook until golden. Turn and finish cooking for 2 minutes. Steam spinach, then toss in a bowl with butter, salt and pepper.

### SALMON AND SAUCE

| | | | | |
|---|---|---|---|---|
| 4 | 6-oz. Atlantic salmon fillets | | 1 T | olive oil |
| 8 oz | bay scallops | | 4 oz | salmon trimmings, diced |
| 2 T | diced shallots | | 1/4 C | dry white wine |
| 3 T | heavy cream | | 1 T | lemon juice |
| 2 t | champagne vinegar | | 1 1/2 T | Frangelico liqueur |
| 1/4 C | toasted, peeled hazelnuts | | | salt and pepper to taste |
| 2 oz | cold butter | | 2 T | chopped fresh parsley |
| | fresh dill for garnish | | | |

Sear salmon in large skillet in oil over high heat, turning when browned and cooking 3 more minutes. Remove and keep warm. Wipe out pan, add shallots, wine, lemon juice, Frangelico and cream, and reduce by half. Add hazelnuts, scallops, salmon trimmings, salt and pepper. Reduce for 2 more minutes and slowly add cold butter, stirring constantly. Remove from heat and add parsley.

### PRESENTATION
Place wild-rice cake in center of plate and put spinach on top. Place salmon alongside. Spoon sauce around cake and partially on salmon. Garnish with fresh dill.

Stubb's

# Broiled Walleye
## With Basil and Pistachio Pesto

*(Serves 4)*

### PESTO

| | | | |
|---|---|---|---|
| ¹/₄ lb | fresh basil | 2 oz | pistachio nuts |
| 1 oz | roasted garlic | 1 t | fresh garlic |
| 1 T | balsamic vinegar | 1 oz | Parmesan cheese |
| 2 oz | extra virgin olive oil | ¹/₈ t | cayenne pepper |
| | salt and freshly cracked black pepper to taste | | |

### WALLEYE

| | | | |
|---|---|---|---|
| 4 | 6-oz. walleye filets | ¹/₂ C | fresh bread crumbs |
| ¹/₄ C | Parmesan cheese | 4 oz | white wine |
| 6 oz | chicken stock | | |

Place all pesto ingredients except oil in a processor and pulse until mixture is a coarse puree. Slowly drizzle in the oil while continuing to process until mixture is emulsified. Preheat oven to 400ºF. Combine wine and stock for use as broiling liquid. Scale walleye filets and remove all pinbones. Place filets, skin side down, in a large, lightly buttered, broiling pan. Avoid any overlap. Spread pesto liberally and evenly over filets, then sprinkle with bread crumbs and Parmesan. Carefully add wine-stock mixture to pan, using just enough to cover the bottom of the pan and the sides of the fish, but not the tops. Place pan in oven at 400ºF for about 8 minutes, then place under low-broil flame until coating is golden and fish is fully cooked.

Top of the Park

# Pan Seared Salmon
### With Black Bean Salsa

*(Serves 4)*

### SALSA

| | | | |
|---|---|---|---|
| 2 | tomatoes, diced | 1 | avocado |
| 2 | jalapeños | 1 | green pepper |
| $1/2$ C | cooked black turtle beans | $1/4$ C | diced red onions |
| 1 T | cilantro | 1 T | key lime juice |
| 1 t | ground cumin | $1/8$ t | salt |
| $1/8$ t | cayenne pepper | | |

Peel and chop avocado. Seed and mince jalapeños. Seed and dice green pepper. Combine all ingredients, cover and refrigerate overnight.

### SALMON

| | | | |
|---|---|---|---|
| 1 lb | salmon | 1 T | butter |
| 2 oz | heavy cream | pinch | saffron |

Heat a sauté pan until hot, add butter. Divide salmon into individual pieces and sear on both sides, turning once, until done. Remove from pan and keep warm. Add heavy cream and saffron, deglaze pan and reduce slightly. To serve, place salmon on salsa and pour cream and pan juice over salmon.

Top of the Park

# Crab Cakes On Glass Noodles
With Red Pepper Cilantro Vinaigrette

*(Serves 6 to 8 as entree or 12 as appetizers)*

## GLASS NOODLE SALAD
(Glass noodles can be found in oriental-food stores or sections)

| | | | |
|---|---|---|---|
| 6 oz | glass noodles, cooked | 3 | cucumbers |
| $^1/_4$ C | brown sugar | 2 oz | rice vinegar |
| $^1/_4$ C | chopped cilantro | 1 oz | sesame oil |
| | salt and pepper to taste | | |

Peel and julienne cucumbers. Combine all ingredients and season with salt and pepper.

## RED PEPPER-CILANTRO VINAIGRETTE

| | | | |
|---|---|---|---|
| 4 | red peppers | $^1/_4$ C | chopped cilantro |
| 1 T | finely chopped garlic | $1^1/_2$ oz | rice vinegar |
| $1^1/_2$ oz | champagne vinegar | 1 C | peanut oil |
| 1 C | olive oil | | salt and pepper to taste |

Roast, peel and devein peppers, puree in food processor, and whisk in remaining ingredients.

## CRAB CAKES

| | | | |
|---|---|---|---|
| 1 lb | lump crabmeat, picked over | 3 | green peppers, finely diced |
| $^1/_2$ C | mayonnaise | 1 oz | Dijon mustard |
| 1 T | garlic, finely chopped | $^1/_2$ C | Italian parsley, chopped |
| $^1/_4$ C | cilantro, chopped | 1 | lemon |
| 4 T | olive oil | 1 C | thin-sliced shiitake mushrooms |
| 20 | Carr's water crackers | | salt, pepper and cayenne to taste |

Sauté sliced mushroom in 1 T of oil. Drain and reserve. Combine mayonnaise, mustard, juice of one lemon, herbs and spices. Add green peppers and mushrooms. Crush water crackers and work into mixture with crabmeat. Form 2-ounce patties and sauté in olive oil until lightly browned. To serve, center glass noodle salad on plates, spoon cilantro vinaigrette on top, and place crab cakes on vinaigrette.

Terry's Place

# Shrimp Scampi

*(Serves 4)*

| | | | |
|---|---|---|---|
| ¹/₄ lb | unsalted butter, softened | 2 T | chopped shallots |
| 2 T | chopped fresh garlic | 2 T | chopped fresh parsley |
| ¹/₂ C | dry white wine | 20 | lg. shrimp (21-25/lb) |
| 1 lb | fettucine or capellini | | salt and pepper to taste |

Cook pasta, drain and set aside. In a medium sauté pan combine 1 T butter, shallots, garlic, parsley and shrimp, and sauté over high heat for about 1 minute. Turn shrimp, add wine and remaining butter, and reduce slightly. Add cooked pasta and toss, making certain all butter has melted and blended thoroughly. Salt and pepper to taste. (*Terry's shrimp scampi is generous; you might find this serves more than four.*)

Terry's Place

# Whitefish Grenobloise

*(Serves 4)*

| | | | |
|---|---|---|---|
| 4 | 6-8 oz. whitefish filet | 8 T | capers |
| 8 T | unsalted butter | 2 t | lemon juice |
| 4 T | chopped fresh parsley | 2 t | chopped shallots |
| | salt, pepper to taste | | |

Sauté whitefish. Combine other ingredients in saucepan and cook over medium high heat until butter has melted. Pour over sautéed fish and serve.

## Walloon Lake Inn

# Rainbow Trout Hemingway

With Lemon Brandy Butter sauce

*(Serves 4)*

| | | | |
|---|---|---|---|
| 4 | 9-oz trout, boned | 6 T | butter |
| 2 T | chopped shallots | 1 C | sliced mushrooms |
| 3 T | fresh lemon juice | 1/4 C | brandy |
| | salt and pepper to taste | | |

Preheat a heavy sauté pan. Add 1T. butter, and when it starts to brown place trout in pan, flesh side down, and brown briefly (2-3 minutes). Repeat for all trout. Place all trout on an oiled cookie sheet and bake at 400ºF until flesh is firm, about 15 minutes. Meanwhile, sauté shallots and mushrooms in butter, add lemon juice and brandy (use care in case the brandy flames). Season with salt and pepper and pour over plated trout. *(The Inn's David Beier says, "It is essential that the trout be fresh. By the time an Idaho trout makes it to Northern Michigan, it's too late. Fresh trout have a slimy touch to their skin.")*

## Weathervane

# Cherry Mustard Shrimp

*(Serves 2)*

| | | | |
|---|---|---|---|
| 2 T | olive oil | 16 | peeled, deveined shrimp |
| 1 | med. carrot | 1 | med. summer squash |
| 1 | med. zucchini | 2 T | Amon Orchards Cherry Mustard |
| 1 C | wild or other rice | | salt, pepper to taste |

Cook rice and hold warm. Julienne zucchini, squash and carrot. Sauté shrimp and vegetables in large pan until vegetables are tender. Add cherry mustard and toss mixture. Rim plate with cooked rice, spoon shrimp mixture inside rice. Garnish with fresh cherries.

Whitney's Oyster Bar

# Shrimp and Chicken Curry

*(Serves 4-6)*

| | | | |
|---|---|---|---|
| 3 T | clarified butter (or oil) | 1 lb | shrimp, shelled & deveined |
| 4 | 8-oz. chicken breasts, cut in strips | 1 | green pepper, seeded and diced |
| 1 | red pepper, seeded and diced | 1 | yellow pepper, seeded and diced |
| 2 | med. carrots, diced | 2 | celery ribs, diced |
| 1 | med. onion, diced | 1 1/2 C | heavy cream |
| 2/3 C | dry white wine | 8 T | raisins or diced apple |
| 8 T | coconut | 3 t | curry powder (or to taste) |
| dash | onion powder, garlic powder, white pepper, paprika, cayenne | | |

Make a spice mixture of curry and a dash each of the spices. In a large skillet, cook the shrimp and chicken in the clarified butter (or oil) for approximately 3 minutes over medium high heat, turning once. Drain oil and add the diced vegetables and wine, stir, and cover to steam vegetables for 4 minutes. Add curry and spice mixture and heavy cream and mix in thoroughly. Increase heat and boil until reduced by half (about 5 minutes). Add coconut and raisins or apple. Serve over rice. The raisins or apple and the coconut can be served in bowls on the side so diners can sprinkle them atop the curried shrimp and chicken as they wish. *(Other side dishes that can be served this way with a curry include crushed peanuts, crumbled bacon, crumbled hard-boiled egg, and mango chutney)*.

Whitney's Oyster Bar

# Whitney's Shrimp
### With Mustard-Chive Chantilly

*(Serves 4)*

## MUSTARD-CHIVE CHANTILLY

| | | | |
|---|---|---|---|
| 1 C | heavy whipping cream | 2 oz | Dijon mustard |
| 2 | egg yolks | 1 T | chives |
| | salt, pepper to taste | | |

Whip cream until it starts to thicken. Add mustard, chive and egg yolks. Whip until very thick, and add salt and pepper. (*Chuck and Gina Whitney warn us that to get this right, you have to "whip forever, or until it is really thick."*)

Shrimp

| | | | |
|---|---|---|---|
| 20 | med. shrimp, peeled and deveined | 3 C | breadcrumbs |
| 4 oz | Old Bay seasoning | 1/2 t | thyme |
| 1/4 t | black pepper | 4 | eggs |
| 1 oz | heavy cream | | |

Peel and devein shrimp. Make a wash of eggs and cream and thoroughly dip shrimp in wash, then dredge in a mixture of breadcrumbs, Old Bay, thyme and pepper. Sauté in hot oil over medium-high flame. remove, drain on a towel, and serve with the mustard-chive chantilly.

## The Authors

# Bourbon Baked Scallops

*(Serves 2)*

| | | | | |
|---|---|---|---|---|
| 1 lb | bay scallops | | $^1/_2$ | med. onion, chopped |
| 2 T | butter | | 1 T | flour |
| $^1/_2$ C | dry sherry | | 6 oz | chicken stock |
| 1 | lemon | | 2 T | bourbon whiskey |
| $^1/_2$ C | dry breadcrumbs | | $^1/_2$ t | paprika |
| $^1/_2$ C | rice, cooked | | | salt, pepper to taste |

Wash, drain and dry scallops. Sauté onion in 1 T. butter and reserve. Melt 1 T. butter in saucepan and blend in flour to make roux. Add sherry, stock, juice of half a lemon, and reserved onion. Season to taste. Simmer 8-10 minutes over low heat, stirring often, to thicken and blend. Stir in bourbon. Remove from heat. Add scallops. Spoon mixture into two individual baking boats, top with breadcrumbs and paprika. Bake 10 minutes at 400°F. Serve over hot rice.

## The Authors

# Shellfish Provençal

*(Serves 4)*

| | | | | |
|---|---|---|---|---|
| $^1/_2$ lb | scallops | | $^1/_2$ lb | shrimp, peeled and deveined |
| 1 | med. onion, chopped | | 1 C | dry vermouth |
| 3 T | unsalted butter | | 4 T | olive oil |
| $^1/_2$ C | grated toast crumbs | | 4 | garlic cloves, crushed |
| 1 t | thyme | | $^1/_2$ C | chopped parsley |

Poach shrimp and scallops in a covered saucepan for one minute with chopped onion and enough wine to cover. Drain and reserve seafood and liquid. Chop shrimp and scallops coarsely (half-inch). In a clean saucepan, heat butter and oil until melted, add half the crumbs and the garlic, thyme, parsley and shellfish. Mix thoroughly. Distribute mixture evenly among individual baking boats. Top with remaining crumbs, sprinkle a few drops oil on each, and spoon on two or three tablespoons of reserved poaching wine. Bake 10 minutes in oven pre-heated to 350°F. Put under broiler at end for a minute to brown. Serve immediately.

## The Authors

# Spiked Smallmouth Bass

*(Serves 4)*

| | | | |
|---|---|---|---|
| 4 | filets of 15-inch bass | 4 | finely crushed saltines |
| 4 T | olive oil | 4 | green onions, finely chopped |
| 1 | garlic clove, crushed | 1 | lemon |
| 2 T | dry vermouth or white wine | 1 T | Spike seasoning |
| ¹/₂ t | paprika | | garlic powder to taste |

Bone and skin filets, wash and blot dry. Mix paprika with crushed saltines and set aside. Sauté onion with crushed garlic in 2 T. oil until soft. Add wine, Spike, juice of half the lemon, and the rest of the oil. Heat to a simmer, pour off and reserve, leaving just enough oil in pan to sauté fish. Sauté filets over medium-high heat, turning once after about three minutes. After turning, sprinkle with crushed cracker mix. Stir reserved sauce well and spoon evenly on top of fish. Add a sprinkling of paprika for color. When fish are done, serve immediately, garnished with slices of remaining lemon. (*Spike, a proprietary mixture of salt, curry and a score of other spices and herbs, is available at such "natural" and "organic" food outlets as Oryana in Traverse City. It is a very savory seasoning, especially for seafood and eggs.*)

The Authors

# Lemon Seafood Pasta
In Garlic Tomato Sauce

*(Serves 4)*

| | | | |
|---|---|---|---|
| $^3/_4$ lb | scallops or shrimp | 3 T | olive oil |
| 1 | med. onion | 1 | rib celery |
| 1 | med. tomato | $^1/_2$ C | fresh parsley |
| 4 | garlic cloves, sliced thin | $^1/_2$ C | chicken stock or broth |
| 1 C | tomato sauce | 1 | lemon (juice only) |
| 1 t | anise seed | $^1/_2$ C | sherry or dry vermouth |
| 2 T | chopped basil leaf | | |
| $^1/_2$ lb | fettucine, penne, farfalle, or other coarse pasta | | |

Chop onion, celery, tomato and parsley. Wash and dry seafood (if large, cut in half-inch pieces), sauté lightly (max. 2 minutes) in 1 T. hot oil. Drain and reserve. In 2 T. oil, lightly sauté the leek, celery, garlic, and tomato. Add chicken stock, anise seed and wine and simmer 5 minutes. Add tomato sauce, parsley, lemon juice and basil and simmer slowly 10 minutes. Prepare pasta, and while it drains, add seafood to sauce to simmer for last 1-2 minutes before plating and saucing the pasta. Garnish with shredded Parmesan and fresh parsley sprigs. *(Feel free to use shrimp, scallops or diced fresh fish. This is a rather liquid dish, best served in soup plates and accompanied by bread.)*

# Beef, Lamb and Pork

Arboretum

## Braised Baby Lamb Racks
With Vegetables and Rosemary

*(Serves 4)*

| | | | |
|---|---|---|---|
| 4 | baby lamb racks | 2 T | olive oil |
| 1 T | chopped garlic | 1 lb | baby carrots |
| 2 T | chopped shallots | 1 T | grainy Dijon mustard |
| 1 lb | sliced mushrooms | 1 C | chopped leek |
| 1 C | dry white wine | 2 | rosemary sprigs |
| 2 T | butter | | salt and pepper to taste |

Pre-heat oven to 350°F. Heat oil in a large sauté pan and pan-fry lamb until lightly browned. Drain excess oil and add vegetables, shallots, garlic, mustard, rosemary and wine. Transfer pan to oven and bake 13 to 15 minutes at 350F. Arrange vegetables and lamb on four plates, reserving pan juices. Add butter to pan juices and emulsify. Add salt and pepper to taste. Spoon generously over lamb and vegetables before serving.

## La Bécasse

# Roast Venison
With Red Wine Sauce

*(Serves 4)*

| | | | |
|---|---|---|---|
| 1 lb | venison | 1 C | red wine |
| 3 oz | cider vinegar | 1 | carrot, chopped |
| 1 | onion, chopped | 2 | stalks celery, chopped |
| 1 | bay leaf | 1 T | thyme |
| 1 T | whole juniper berries | 1 T | whole coriander |
| 1 T | whole allspice | 1 T | whole black peppercorns |

Combine ingredients and marinate meat in the refrigerator for 48 hours. Remove meat from marinade, reserving marinade. Dry meat and sauté until brown, then roast in oven at 350°F until done as desired. Bring marinade to boil, reduce by half, adding additional wine and seasoning to taste. Use as sauce.

## Hose House Deli

# Stifatho Stew

*(Serves 8)*

| | | | |
|---|---|---|---|
| 3 lb | lamb, diced for stew | 1 | lg. onion, finely chopped |
| 3 oz | olive oil | 2 T | wine vinegar |
| 8 oz | red wine | 1 | lg. garlic clove |
| 1 pt | chopped fresh tomatoes w/juice | 1 | bay leaf |
| | salt and pepper to taste | 1 pt | hot water |
| 3 lb | pearl onions | 1 T | butter |

Heat oil in a large stew pot, and lightly brown lamb and chopped onion. Add remaining ingredients and cook over medium heat until meat is tender. In a separate pan, brown small onions in butter and add to stew. Continue cooking stew slowly until onions are soft. Serve and say: "Yasoo!!" (*The Hose House's Sam Secson tells us that this recipe will make enough stew for "eight small Greeks, or six large ones."*)

## Bowers Harbor Inn

# Tournedoes Santa Fe
### With Sea Scallops

*(Serves 4)*

TOURNEDOES

| | | | |
|---|---|---|---|
| 8 | 4-oz. beef tenderloin filets | 4 oz | onion julienne |
| 1 | chipotle chili, minced | 1 C | tomato concasse |
| 4 oz | butter | ¹/₂ C | Marsala wine |
| 4 t | minced parsley | 12 | sea scallops |

SOUTHWESTERN RUB

| | | | |
|---|---|---|---|
| 4 t | salt | ¹/₄ C | granulated sugar |
| ¹/₄ C | brown sugar | ¹/₄ C | ground cumin |
| ¹/₄ C | chili powder | ¹/₂ C | paprika |
| ¹/₄ C | coarsely-ground black pepper | | |

Char-grill scallops and reserve, kept warm. Mix all "Southwestern Rub" ingredients well and rub filets, then sear in very hot sauté pan. Add onions, chilis and tomatoes, then splash mixture with Marsala and butter, finish with minced parsley. Arrange filets on plate, top with sauce from pan, and top that with char-grilled scallops.

## The New York

# Wolverine Pork Loin

*(Serves 6)*

| | | | |
|---|---|---|---|
| 2¹/₂ lb | center cut pork loin | 8 oz | cooked wild rice |
| 8 oz | dried tart cherries | 2 T | olive oil |
| | rosemary and thyme to taste | | salt and pepper to taste |

Trim and discard pork fat. Square off ends of the loin and grind or process the scraps. Make a stuffing by thoroughly mixing the ground scraps in a bowl with wild rice, cherries, salt, pepper and herbs. Butterfly and pound out the pork loin. Lay stuffing down the middle of the loin, then roll up the sides and tie with butcher's twine. Brush rolled pork with oil, season with salt and pepper, and bake at 375°F. for about 45 minutes. Let cool five minutes before slicing. Serve with pan gravy.

Tapawingo

# Pan-roasted Beef Medallions
## With Wild Mushroom Hash and Truffled Madeira Sauce

*(Serves 4)*

## BEEF MEDALLIONS

| | | | |
|---|---|---|---|
| 4 | 1 1/2 in. beef tenderloin medallions | 2 T | olive oil |
| 2 | cloves garlic, chopped | | |
| 1 1/2 T | chopped fresh rosemary, sage, thyme, parsley | | |
| | coarsely ground black pepper to taste | | |

Cover beef with oil, herbs and garlic, wrap in film and refrigerate overnight. Sprinkle with pepper and sear over high heat in sauté pan with small amount of oil until richly browned (about 2 minutes a side). Salt lightly and roast in 400 F oven for 5 minutes (medium rare). Let rest 5 minutes in warm place before serving.

## MUSHROOM HASH

| | | | |
|---|---|---|---|
| 4 C | assorted wild mushrooms | 1 T | brown butter |
| 1 | small shallot, minced | 1/3 | small onion, diced |
| 1/4 C | dry white wine | 1 C | diced, blanched potatoes |
| 2 T | veal demi-glace | | |
| 2 t | chopped herbs (thyme, sage, chives, Italian parsley) | | |
| | salt and coarsely ground pepper to taste | | |

Wash and coarsely chop mushrooms and sauté in just enough brown butter until lightly browned. Stir in shallot and onion and continue until onion is almost transparent. Deglaze pan with wine and fold in herbs and potato. Moisten with demi-glace and season.

## MADEIRA SAUCE

| | | | |
|---|---|---|---|
| 1 | lg. shallot, peeled, chopped | 1 | bay leaf |
| 1 | sprig fresh thyme | 4 | black peppercorns |
| 4 C | brown veal stock | 2 T | chopped black truffle peelings |
| 2 t | butter | 3 T | Madeira |
| | white truffle oil | | |

In a small saucepan sweat the shallot, bay, thyme and peppercorns. Add the stock, bring to simmer and slowly reduce to half. In separate pan, sweat the truffle peelings in butter.

Add the Madeira and reduce to half. Strain the veal sauce into the truffle mixture. Adjust seasonings and whisk in extra butter if desired.

## PRESENTATION
Spoon 3 oz. of hash in center of heated dinner plate. Place beef medallion on top. Spoon 1/4 C. Madeira sauce around perimeter of hash. Drizzle a teaspoon of white truffle oil over the sauce. Garnish each plate with 4 spears of steamed, buttered asparagus and 3 braised pearl onions.

Stafford's Pier

# Veal Dijon

*(Serves 4)*

| | | | |
|---|---|---|---|
| 8 | veal medallions | 1 T | butter or oil |
| 6 oz | button mushrooms, minced | $^1/_4$C | minced green onion |
| 1 qt. | heavy cream | 2 T | pale sherry |
| 1$^1/_2$T | whole grain Dijon mustard | 4 T | smooth Dijon mustard |
| | salt, pepper to taste | | |

Pound veal and sauté in oil or butter. Remove and keep warm. Sauté mushrooms and onion in a little oil to make *duxelles* (paste). Add sherry and reduce until almost dry. Reserve. Heat cream in a pan to a low boil and reduce to 3/4 of its original volume (if thicker sauce is wanted, reduce more, or thicken with roux). Stir in duxelles and mustards, season with salt and pepper, and serve over veal. (*This recipe makes about a quart of sauce. Stafford's restaurants also use this sauce on chicken and beef. Adding mustards and duxelles to mayonnaise instead of reduced cream makes a cold sauce.*)

Trillium

# Veal Medallions Boursin
on Sautéed Spinach with Red Currant Juice

*(Serves 4)*

| | | | |
|---|---|---|---|
| 4 T | butter | 5 T | minced shallots |
| 2 C | red wine | 1 gal | beef or veal stock |
| 1 C | red currant jelly | 1½ lb | boneless veal loin. |
| 3 T | olive oil | ¾ lb | fresh stemmed spinach |
| ¼ C | white wine | 6 oz | Boursin or herbed cream cheese |

## SAUCE

Sauté 3T. of shallots in 2 T. butter. When translucent, add the red wine and reduce by half. Add stock and reduce to desired thickness. Add red currant jelly and simmer over low heat. ( If you substitute beef broth for stock, thicken it with cornstarch slurry instead of reducing it.)

## VEAL AND SPINACH

Cut veal into 2-oz. medallions. Bring oil to high heat in a large sauté pan, add veal and brown on both sides, then remove from pan. Add remaining shallots and butter to pan and when hot add spinach leaves and sauté lightly. Add white wine and stir to deglaze pan, and remove pan from heat.

## PRESENTATION

Divide Boursin in four equal pieces and pound each piece to a flat disk (it helps if cheese is between sheets of parchment paper). Pour 2-3 oz. of sauce in center of each plate. Arrange sautéed spinach on sauce. Place Boursin disks on spinach, and shingle the veal on top.

## Windows

# Firecracker Pork

*(Serves 4)*

| | | | | |
|---|---|---|---|---|
| 1 lb | pork tenderloin | | 1 t | minced shallot |
| 1 T | minced garlic | | $^1/_2$ C | tamari |
| $^1/_4$ C | sesame oil | | 1 | carrot |
| 2 | stalks celery | | 1 | bunch leeks |
| $^1/_2$ t | cayenne pepper | | 1 t | minced ginger |
| 1 C | beef or chicken stock | | $^1/_2$ C | toasted cashews |
| | salt and pepper to taste | | $^1/_2$ lb | bow-tie pasta, cooked |

Peel and julienne carrot, celery, and leeks. Clean pork of fat and sinew. Cut into $^1/_2$-inch slices. Make a marinade of all ingredients except stock and cashews, and marinate pork 24 hours. Sauté pork until smoky in a hot skillet or wok with 1 T. sesame oil and marinade mixture. Add beef or chicken stock. Simmer for 10 minutes and serve over bow-tie pasta garnished with toasted cashews.

## The Authors

# Grilled Lemon-Curry Sirloin

*(Serves 4)*

| | | | | |
|---|---|---|---|---|
| 4-10-oz | 3/4" strip sirloins | | 1 T | curry powder |
| 1 | lemon, juice only | | 1 t | thyme |
| | salt, pepper to taste | | | |

Bring steaks to room temperature. An hour before grilling, sprinkle lightly with half the lemon juice, then rub liberally with salt and pepper and sprinkle lightly with thyme and liberally with curry powder on both sides. Grill to desired doneness, turning once. A few moments before removing from fire, sprinkle again with remaining lemon juice. Let rest briefly before serving.

# The Authors

# Brother Phil's Barbecue

(Serves 24)

| | | | | |
|---|---|---|---|---|
| 10 lbs | pork | 1 gal. | Red & White BBQ sauce |
| 2 | large white onions, diced | $^1/_3$ lb | brown sugar |
| 1 | No. 10 can tomato juice | | Lawry's Seasoning Salt |
| 1 bottle | Manitou Amber Ale | | |

Rub pork with seasoning salt, wrap in foil in two 5-pound parcels, and roast slowly until meat reaches 180°F. In a large pot, combine barbecue sauce, onion, brown sugar and tomato juice and simmer 1 hour. Unwrap foil and drain all juices into simmering sauce. Finely shred the pork, stir it into sauce, and simmer another half hour so sauce thoroughly penetrates shredded pork. Refrigerate until needed, then re-heat. If barbecue is too thick, thin it with ale while heating. (*Brother Phil Lovelace does this BBQ at family picnics, and the recipe probably makes more sauce than you'll need because Phil does a whole hog, foil-wrapped in 5-pound lots and cooked four hours in a charcoal roaster the size of the Queen Mary. Use whatever cuts you want with enough fat to yield juice and meat lean enough to shred. Red and White, "Show-Me" brand or any good, smoky sauce will do. Phil uses Bud to thin his sauce, but only because they don't sell Manitou Amber where he lives.*)

# Poultry

La Bécasse

## Chicken and Chèvre en Papillote

(Amounts are per serving)

| | | | |
|---|---|---|---|
| 1 | boneless, skinless chicken breast | | parchment paper |
| | butter | $^1/_2$ C | cooked wild rice |
| $^1/_2$ C | sautéed sliced mushrooms | $^1/_2$ C | thinly sliced leeks |
| 3 | slices chèvre | 1 T | pine nuts |
| 2 T | dry white wine | pinch | each tarragon, basil, and thyme |
| 1 | artichoke heart, cut into quarters | | |

Pound chicken breast thin. Cut parchment paper into large heart shapes. Fold in half. Brush inside with butter. Place wild rice on half the paper heart, sprinkle on sautéed mushrooms and place half the chicken breast on top. Arrange leeks and chèvre on chicken. Sprinkle with pine nuts, wine, tarragon, basil, and thyme. Cover with remaining half of chicken breast. Arrange hearts of artichoke around the edges. Fold the top half of the paper heart over and seal by making small folds toward the top of the paper, rotating and creasing each fold. Fold the point of the heart under last. Bake on a sheet pan for 30 minutes at 325ºF or until chicken is tender. To serve, remove top of paper with scissors and serve the chicken in the paper. (Baking time will vary, depending on size and thickness of breasts).

La Cuisine Amical

# Chicken Pot Pie

*(Serves 8)*

| | | | | |
|---|---|---|---|---|
| 4 C | diced, cooked chicken | | 1 C | peeled, diced carrot |
| 2 C | diced celery | | 1 | med. onion, peeled & diced |
| 1 C | frozen green peas | | 1 lb | potato |
| 1 C | sliced mushrooms | | 2 C | whipping cream |
| 2 C | milk | | 2 T | chervil |
| 2 T | dried basil | | $1/2$ T | salt |
| $1/2$ T | pepper | | 1 T | chicken base |
| 4 oz | margarine | | $1/2$ C | all-purpose flour |
| $1/4$ C | grated Parmesan | | | |

Peel, dice and cook potatoes. Preheat oven to 375°F. Sauté vegetables in margarine in bottom of small stock pot. When onion is translucent, add flour and mix thoroughly. Simmer 5 minutes, stirring. Add milk, cream, potato, spices, chicken base and Parmesan. Heat until sauce has thickened. Add roux if needed to thicken more. Check for seasoning. Place filling in a baking boat or dish and cover with puff pastry dough. Bake at 375°F for 10-12 minutes.

# Grilled Chicken Breast
## With Strawberry Barbecue Sauce

*(Serves 8)*

| | | | |
|---|---|---|---|
| 8 | chicken breasts, char-grilled | ²/₃ C | chopped onion |
| 3 t | chopped garlic | 1¹/₃ T | sesame oil |
| ¹/₃ C | water | ¹/₃ C | cider vinegar |
| 2²/₃ T | catsup | ¹/₃ C | strained strawberry preserves |
| 1¹/₃ T | light molasses | 2 t | Worcestershire sauce |
| ²/₃ C | strawberries | dash | red pepper |
| ¹/₃ t | ground ginger | 1 t | whole cumin seeds |
| 2²/₃ T | brown sugar | | |

Sauté onion and garlic in sesame oil until tender. Add other ingredients and spices and simmer 30 minutes. (*Hattie's Jim Milliman refers to this as a "basic" barbecue sauce and suggests, "You can substitute any fruit" for the strawberry. He also suggests using it to sauce grilled pork as well as chicken.*)

Monte Bianco

# Rollatini di Pollo

*(Serves 4)*

### WHITE CREAM SAUCE

| | | | | |
|---|---|---|---|---|
| 1¹/₂ t | chopped garlic | | 1 T | olive oil |
| 1¹/₂ pt | heavy cream | | dash | nutmeg |
| pinch | white pepper | | | salt to taste |

Cover bottom of heavy pot with olive oil and wilt garlic over medium heat. Add cream, nutmeg and pepper, whisk, and reduce to desired consistency (it should remain fairly free flowing). Season with salt to taste, strain and reserve.

### ROLLATINI

| | | | | |
|---|---|---|---|---|
| 4 | boneless, skinless chicken breasts | | 1 t | olive oil |
| 4 | very thin slices prosciutto | | 4 | thin slices mozzarella |
| 4 | figs, sliced thin | | 2 T | Gorgonzola |

### MEAT GLAZE

Wash and dry chicken breasts and trim excess fat. Butterfly breasts and pound to about 1/4-inch thickness. Layer prosciutto, mozzarella and fig slices on breasts, tuck in sides of breast and roll. Wrap securely in plastic wrap and chill until firm (at least one hour). Place in lightly oiled baking dish in oven preheated to 350ºF and bake until firm to touch, about 20 or 30 minutes. Heat white cream sauce in heavy skillet. Add Gorgonzola and your favorite meat glaze. Cook over medium flame until cheese melts and sauce flows fairly freely. Slice chicken breasts on diagonal and fan on warm plates. Pour sauce around edges of chicken. *(Monte Bianco's John and Mary Kelly like to serve this with roasted redskin potatoes and a fresh, steamed, seasonal vegetable.)*

## Old Mission Tavern

# Chicken Breast Artichoke

*(Serves 2)*

| | | | |
|---|---|---|---|
| 2 | 6-ounce chicken breasts | 2 T | butter |
| ¹/₂ C | flour | 8 oz | artichoke hearts |
| 3 to 4 | chopped green onions, tops and white | | |
| 3 oz | sliced shiitake mushrooms | 4 oz | white wine |
| 1 t | chicken base | 1 C | heavy cream |
| ³/₄ T | ground fresh garlic | | salt and pepper to taste |

Dredge chicken in flour seasoned with salt and pepper, then sauté in butter until done but not dry (about 4 minutes a side). Set aside and keep warm. To skillet, add artichoke hearts, chopped green onions, mushrooms, and sauté 2 minutes (add butter if necessary). Add white wine, chicken base and cream. Reduce until thickened. Pour over chicken breast. Serve with rice or linguine.

## Reflections

# Apple Chutney Chicken

*(Serves 8)*

| | | | |
|---|---|---|---|
| 8 | boneless chicken breasts | 4 | apples |
| 2 T | minced red onion | ¹/₂ C | dried cherries |
| ³/₄ C | brown sugar | 3 oz | cider vinegar |
| 1 t | pumpkin pie spice | 2 t | curry powder |

Charbroil chicken breasts. Core and dice apples. Combine apples with other ingredients and cook over low heat until apples are soft and liquid is absorbed. Serve breasts with apple chutney.

The Authors

# Roast Cornish Hen
## With Orange-garlic Sauce

*(Serves 2)*

| | | | |
|---|---|---|---|
| 2 | Cornish hens | 2 T | olive oil |
| 1 t | lemon pepper | 1 t | garlic powder |
| 1 t | crushed savory leaf | 1 t | rubbed sage |
| 3 T | butter | ½ C | orange juice |
| 1 t | honey | 3 T | dry white wine |
| 2 | cloves garlic, crushed | | |

Wash hens and pat dry. Brush with oil and sprinkle with lemon pepper, garlic powder, savory leaf and sage. For sauce, melt butter in a small saucepan, add orange juice, honey, wine and garlic. Stir and simmer a few minutes. Roast hens 45 minutes at 350°F, basting every 10 minutes with sauce. Reserve some sauce to add before serving.

# Vegetarian & Pasta

## Cafe Bliss

## Sesame Veggie Pasta
With Sautéed Tofu and Spicy Peanut Sauce

### PEANUT SAUCE

| | | | |
|---|---|---|---|
| 1 C | crunchy peanut butter | 2 T | honey |
| 1-2 t | Chinese hot paste (ground Thai peppers in oil) | | |
| 2 T | tamari | 2 T | minced garlic |
| 1/2 t | freshly ground black pepper | 1 C | roasted sesame seeds |
| 2 T | tahini | 1 T | rice vinegar |
| 1 C | water | | |

Process ingredients until creamy, reserving some sesame seeds.

### VEGGIE TOFU PASTA

| | | | |
|---|---|---|---|
| 1 lb | angel hair or linguine | 1 lb | tofu |
| 3 T | tamari | 1 t | orange zest |
| 1 t | garlic powder | 1 t | onion powder |
| 1 t | ginger | 1 t | poultry seasoning |
| | water | | |
| | assorted chopped vegetables (broccoli, carrots, peppers, cabbage, mushrooms, snow peas, red and green onion | | |

Cut tofu into 1-inch cubes. Marinate overnight in a mixture of the remaining ingredients and enough water to cover the tofu. When ready to serve, cook and drain pasta. Sauté tofu and add cut vegetables. Arrange on bed of freshly cooked pasta, top with peanut sauce, sesame seeds and green onion.

Carriage House,   Hotel Iroquois

# Fettucine Alfredo with Morels

*(Serves 4)*

| | | | |
|---|---|---|---|
| 1/4 lb | butter | 1 C | heavy cream |
| 1 T | Cognac | 1 1/4 lb | fresh morels |
| 1 lb | fettucine | 1/2 C | freshly grated Parmesan |
| | salt, pepper to taste | | |

Rinse and drain morels and pat dry. (If you use dried morels, use 1/4 pound and reconstitute). Melt 2 T of the butter in a skillet over moderately low heat. Add cream, Cognac, salt and pepper, and bring to a boil. Add morels and simmer, covered, for 10 minutes. Set aside and keep warm. Cook the fettucine al dente in boiling salted water, then drain. In a large skillet, melt the remaining butter, add the pasta and the morel mixture and Parmesan. Season to taste and toss well. Serve on heated plates with additional Parmesan. (*This is served at the Carriage House as an appetizer, in which case it is sufficient for 6-8 servings.*)

Monte Bianco

# Tortellini Verdi e Bianchi

*(Serves 4)*

## WHITE CREAM SAUCE

| | | | |
|---|---|---|---|
| 1 $^1/_2$ t | chopped garlic | 1 $^1/_2$ pt | heavy cream |
| dash | nutmeg | pinch | white pepper |
| | salt to taste | | |

Cover bottom of heavy pot with olive oil and wilt garlic. Add cream, nutmeg and pepper. Whisk until desired consistency is reached (it should be fairly free-flowing). Season with salt to taste, strain and reserve.

## TORTELLINI

| | | | |
|---|---|---|---|
| 20 oz | cheese-filled spinach tortellini | 2 oz | imported prosciutto, julienned |
| 4 T | sweet butter | 6 T | roasted pine nuts |
| $^1/_2$ C | half-and-half | 2 T | freshly chopped parsley |

Boil tortellini in 4 quarts of water until done. While tortellini is cooking, sauté prosciutto in small amount of olive oil until crisp but not brown. Strain excess oil. Add cream sauce and butter and cook down until slightly reduced. (Thin with a little half-and-half if necessary.) Add drained tortellini to mixture and toss. Apportion on 4 heated plates. Garnish with pine nuts and freshly chopped parsley. Serve with freshly grated Parmesan cheese and freshly ground black pepper. (Note: It is easier to use two large skillets with equal portions, serving two portions from each skillet.)

## Old Mission Tavern

# Blue Cheese Spinach Pasta
With Bacon

*(Serves 2)*

| | | | |
|---|---|---|---|
| 3 | strips bacon | 3 T | olive oil |
| 1 | clove garlic, chopped | dash | black pepper |
| 2 C | spinach (fresh) | 3 C | cooked linguine |
| 2 T | blue cheese (crumbled) | 1/4 C | Parmesan |
| 1/2 C | mozzarella (shredded) | | |

Cook and crumble the bacon and reserve. Sauté garlic in oil until lightly brown. Add pepper and spinach, and stir until well wilted. Add linguine, Parmesan and mozzarella. Toss until cheese is melted. Place in serving dish and top with blue cheese. Run under broiler about one minute. Add crumbled bacon and serve with garlic bread or plain sour dough roll.

## Paparazzi

# Lasagna

*(Serves 4)*

| | | | |
|---|---|---|---|
| 4 | lasagna dough sheets, cooked & drained | | |
| 1 C | ricotta cheese | 1 | egg |
| 1 C | shredded Fontina cheese | 1/2 C | grated Parmesan |
| 1/2 C | Italian sausage, cooked & crumbled | 1/2 C | julienned capicolla |
| 1/2 C | julienned prosciutto | 2 C | pasta sauce |
| | basil, oregano, Italian parsley to taste | | |

In a medium bowl, thoroughly mix egg, ricotta, and herbs. Set aside. Lay pasta sheets on counter. Spread ricotta mixture evenly on all four sheets, and distribute meats and cheeses evenly on top. Roll up pasta sheets fairly loosely, end to end (if rolled too tight they will take longer to heat through in oven). Place rolls in sprayed baking dish, top each with pasta sauce (use whatever sauce you prefer), and bake 15 minutes at 375°F. Midway through baking, top with some additional Parmesan, if you wish. (*Capicolla, a fatty Italian ham, is available at Folgarelli's in Traverse City*).

The Rowe

# Wild Mushroom Penne

(Serves 6)

| | | | |
|---|---|---|---|
| 1 C | coarsely chopped onion | 1 C | coarsely-chopped cabbage |
| 3 | garlic cloves, minced | 1/2 C | butter |
| 2 t | thyme leaves | 1 t | tarragon |
| 1 C | vegetable stock | 1/2 lb | shiitake mushrooms |
| 1/2 lb | button mushrooms | 1/2 lb | morels |
| 1/4 lb | Portobello mushrooms | 3 C | heavy cream |
| 1 C | grated Parmesan cheese | 1 lb | penne pasta |
| 1/4 C | chopped parsley | | |

Wash mushrooms. Quarter button mushrooms and slice shiitake and Portobello mushrooms. Sauté all mushrooms in butter, and set aside. Melt butter in a skillet and sauté onion and cabbage until softened (about 7 minutes). Add garlic, thyme, tarragon and vegetable stock and simmer together another 10 minutes. Cook and drain penne. Reduce cream in a large, heavy saucepan until thickened. Add the mushrooms, pasta and cheese and mix thoroughly. Season with salt and freshly ground pepper. Sprinkle with chopped parsley. Serve immediately.

# Desserts

## American Spoon Foods

## Independence Cake

| | | | | |
|---|---|---|---|---|
| 2¹/₂ C | all-purpose flour | | ¹/₂ t | cinnamon |
| 1 t | freshly grated nutmeg | | ¹/₂ t | double-acting baking powder |
| 1 C | sweet butter | | 1¹/₂ C | granulated sugar |
| 4 | lg. eggs (room temperature) | | 1 t | vanilla extract |
| 1 t | baking soda | | 1 C | buttermilk |
| 1 jar | blueberry Spoon Fruit™ | | 1 jar | sour cherry Spoon Fruit™ |
| 1 T | confectioners' sugar | | | |

Preheat oven to 350°F. Grease three, round, 9-inch cake pans and line them with parchment paper. Sift flour, cinnamon, nutmeg and baking powder together in one bowl. In a large mixing bowl, cream the butter and gradually add granulated sugar, blending well. Beat in the eggs, one at a time, until mixture is light and fluffy. Add vanilla and blend well. Dissolve baking soda in buttermilk in a small bowl. Beginning and ending with the flour mixture, alternately add flour mixture and buttermilk mixture to the butter mixture. Divide batter into prepared pans and bake in preheated oven for 20-25 minutes or until edges begin to pull away from sides of pans and center springs back when pressed lightly. Cool in pans for 10 minutes, then turn out onto wire racks and cool completely. Spread bottom layer with blueberry Spoon Fruit, set middle layer on top and spread with sour cherry Spoon Fruit. Put on top layer and sift confectioners' sugar onto it. (*This recipe is from Chris Chickering, research-and-development chef at American Spoon Foods.*)

Andante

# Apple Cobbler
## With Dried Cherry and Cashew Biscuit Topping

*(Serves 10-12)*

### FILLING

| | | | | |
|---|---|---|---|---|
| $^2/_3$ C | sugar | | $^1/_4$ C | flour |
| 1 t | cinnamon | | 16 | apples, peeled, cored & sliced |
| $^1/_2$ C | corn syrup | | 1 T | lemon juice |
| 1 oz | butter | | | |

Butter a 9x13 glass baking dish. In a bowl, combine sugar, flour and cinnamon. Mix in apples, corn syrup, lemon juice. Push mixture into baking dish, dot with butter and bake 45 minutes at 400°F.

### TOPPING

| | | | | |
|---|---|---|---|---|
| $1^2/_3$ C | flour | | $^1/_2$ C | cashews |
| $^1/_2$ C | dried cherries | | $^1/_4$ C | sugar |
| 1 T | baking powder | | $^1/_2$ t | cardamom |
| 3 oz | butter | | 1 C | whipping cream |

In a processor, grind all ingredients except butter and cream. Pulse in the butter, then the cream. Spread mixture on hot filling and return to oven about 25 minutes, or until tester comes out clean. Serve with vanilla ice cream and warm caramel sauce.

### CARAMEL SAUCE

| | | | | |
|---|---|---|---|---|
| $1^1/_3$ C | whipping cream | | 1 C | sugar |
| 3 T | water | | 1 oz | butter |

Bring whipping cream to simmer and set aside. Combine sugar and water and stir over medium heat to dissolve sugar, then turn heat high and boil without stirring until caramel is deep amber. Lower heat. Stir in whipping cream slowly until mixture is smooth. Remove from heat and stir in butter.

## Stafford's Bay View Inn

# Lemon Bars

| | | | | |
|---|---|---|---|---|
| 2 C | flour | | $^1/_2$ C | powdered sugar |
| $^1/_2$ lb | butter | | $1^1/_2$ C | granulated sugar |
| 1 t | baking powder | | 3 | eggs |
| $^1/_4$ C | lemon juice | | 1 T | grated lemon peel |

Mix flour, powdered sugar and butter thoroughly and press into a well-oiled, heavy-duty cookie sheet. Bake at 350ºF for 20 minutes. Combine remaining ingredients and whip thoroughly, the pour over baked crust and bake another 25 minutes at 350ºF. Dust with powdered sugar if desired. Cool until set. Cut and serve.

## La Bécasse

# Hazelnut Pudding

*(Serves 10)*

| | | | | |
|---|---|---|---|---|
| $^1/_2$ lb | butter | | $^2/_3$ C | confectioners' sugar |
| 6 | eggs, separated | | 1 oz | brandy |
| $^1/_2$ C | granulated sugar | | 6 oz | toasted, ground hazelnuts |
| 5 oz | dry breadcrumbs | | dash | salt |

Butter ten 6-ounce ramekins. Cream butter with confectioners' sugar. Beat in egg yolks one at a time. Beat in brandy. In a separate bowl, beat egg whites until foamy. Gradually beat in granulated sugar. Fold toasted nuts, bread crumbs and salt into the creamed butter mixture. Add $^1/_3$ of the egg white. Continue folding. Fold in remaining egg whites. Turn mixture into ramekins and cover each with foil. Place in water bath and bake at 350ºF until puddings are firm, about 35 minutes. To serve, turn warm puddings out of ramekin onto plates, sprinkle with confectioners' sugar and garnish with *crème Anglaise*, fresh strawberries and lingonberry jam.

La Bécasse

# White Chocolate Mousse
With Raspberry Sauce

*(Serves 8)*

| | | | |
|---|---|---|---|
| ¹/₄ C | half-and-half | 2 T | white creme de cacao |
| 9 oz | white chocolate, coarsely chopped | 3 | egg whites |
| 1¹/₂ C | heavy cream | 1 t | vanilla |
| dash | cream of tartar | 2 C | fresh raspberries |
| | sugar | | lemon juice |
| | club soda | | |

Combine half-and-half, creme de cacao and white chocolate in the top of a double boiler and stir constantly over boiling water just until melted. Remove from heat and stir occasionally until cool. Beat egg whites with cream of tartar until soft peaks form. Fold egg whites into chocolate mixture. Beat cream until firm. Fold whipped cream and vanilla into chocolate mixture. Divide into eight serving dishes. To make sauce, puree fresh raspberries, strain, and adjust to taste and consistency with sugar, lemon juice and club soda.

Bowers Harbor Inn

# Fresh Fruit Flan

*(Makes one 12-inch flan—about 8 servings)*

## CRUST

| | | | |
|---|---|---|---|
| 4 oz | cream cheese, softened | ¹/₂C | margarine |
| 1¹/₄C | flour | ¹/₄ t | salt |

Combine cream cheese and margarine, mixing until well blended. Add flour and salt and mix well. Form into ball and chill at least one hour. On a lightly floured surface, roll into a 14-inch circle and place in a 12-inch tart pan. Prick side and bottom with a fork. Bake at 375ºF until golden (about 8-10 minutes). Cool completely, then remove from tart pan to a baker's sheet.

## FILLING

| | | | |
|---|---|---|---|
| 12 oz | cream cheese softened | ¹/₃ C | sugar |
| 1 T | lemon juice | 1 C | whipping cream |
| | fresh, seasonal fruit or berries | | |

Whip cream. Combine cream cheese, sugar and lemon juice in a bowl and mix well. Remove to a large, stainless-steel bowl. Fold in whipped cream. Spoon filling into crust and spread evenly. Arrange fresh fruit on top.

## GLAZE

| | | | |
|---|---|---|---|
| 1 T | water | ¹/₂ C | apricot preserves |

Add water to preserves and mix 5-10 seconds at high speed in blender (do not mix longer, or mixture will foam). Drizzle glaze over fruit on top of flan. Chill flan well.

# Grand Hotel

# Fudge Sauce

*(Makes 1-1/2 quarts)*

| | | | |
|---|---|---|---|
| $^1/_4$ lb | butter | 1 lb | powdered sugar |
| $^1/_4$ C | heavy cream (or 1 can evap. milk) | $^1/_4$ lb | milk chocolate |
| $^1/_4$ lb | bitter chocolate | $^1/_8$ t | salt |
| 1 t | vanilla extract | | |

In the top of a double boiler heat all ingredients except vanilla and cook for 30 minutes, stirring frequently. Cool the sauce and beat in the vanilla.

# Grand Hotel

# Rum Sauce

| | | | |
|---|---|---|---|
| 1 lb | dark brown sugar | $^1/_2$ lb | butter, melted |
| 2 | lemons (juice and zest) | 1 t | rum extract |
| 2 | eggs | | |

In the top of a double boiler, combine all ingredients except rum extract, heat and beat until liquid and thick. Add the rum extract and mix in thoroughly. Serve immediately, over pie or ice cream. Refrigerate unused portion and store in refrigerator; reheat before serving. *(This is the recipe of W. Stewart Woodfill, owner of Grand Hotel in the 1940s and '50s and one of the key architects of modern Mackinac Island's tourist industry.)*

# Grand Hotel

# Sacher Torte

<hr>

TORTE

| | | | |
|---|---|---|---|
| 2 C | granulated sugar | 2 C | flour |
| ¹/₄ C | cocoa | ¹/₄ lb | butter |
| 1 C | water | ¹/₂ C | corn oil |
| 2 | lg. eggs | ¹/₂ C | buttermilk |
| 1¹/₂ t | baking soda | 1 t | vanilla |
| 1 C | apricot marmalade, pureed | | |

Thoroughly combine sugar, cocoa, and flour in a mixing bowl. In a heavy saucepan, heat the butter, water and oil together and bring to a boil. Add to the dry mixture and blend well. Add the eggs and blend in thoroughly. Add the buttermilk, baking soda, vanilla and mix in well. Pour mixture into a greased, floured, 9-inch cake pan and bake 50-60 minutes at 350ºF or until a toothpick inserted in cake comes out clean. remove from oven and let cool in the pan 20 minutes, then turn out onto a rack and let cool completely.

GANACHE (icing)

| | | | |
|---|---|---|---|
| 16 oz | semi-sweet chocolate | 1¹/₂ C | heavy cream |

Put the chocolate into a heat-proof mixing bowl. Bring the cream to a boil over medium-high heat in a small, heavy saucepan. Pour hot cream over the chocolate and whisk until all chocolate is melted and mixture is smooth. Let cool until mixture is just warm to the touch but still pourable. (The ganache can be prepared two or three days ahead and stored, covered, in the refrigerator. To soften for use, place the bowl in a pan of hot water over low heat and stir until smooth and pourable.)

ASSEMBLY

Split the cooled cake into three even layers. Spread the top of each layer with apricot marmalade puree and stack the three layers. Use remaining puree to cover the sides of the torte. Place the torte in the freezer for an hour. When cake is cold, place on a rack over a large sheet pan, and ladle the warm ganache over the torte, using a spatula if needed to make smooth. (To make this a truly authentic Sacher Torte, write the word "Sacher" on the cake with melted, semi-sweet chocolate from a pastry bag.) Serve with whipped cream.

La Cuisine Amical

# Super Chocolate Chip Cookies

*(Makes 12 large cookies)*

| | | | |
|---|---|---|---|
| 1 C | softened butter | $^7/_8$ C | sugar |
| $^7/_8$ C | brown sugar | 1/4 C | corn syrup |
| 2 | lg. eggs | 1 t | vanilla extract |
| 2 C | all-purpose flour | $2^1/_2$ C | oatmeal |
| $^1/_2$ t | salt | 1 t | baking powder |
| 1 t | baking soda | 3 oz | grated semi-sweet chocolate |
| $^3/_4$ lb | semi-sweet chocolate chips | | |

Preheat oven to 325°F. In a mixer, cream the butter, sugars, corn syrup, eggs and vanilla. In a separate bowl, sift the flour, salt, baking powder, and baking soda. Combine the contents of the bowls and add oatmeal. Mix thoroughly. Add chocolate chips and the grated chocolate. Transfer with a scoop (#8 size) to a parchment-lined full-sheet pan. Press down slightly. Bake at 325°F for 14-18 minutes, rotating the pan at least once to assure even baking.

Monte Bianco

# Apple Pizza

*(Serves 4)*

| | | | |
|---|---|---|---|
| 2 | lg. Granny Smith apples | 2 T | brown sugar |
| 1 T | water | | granulated sugar |
| | bakers cinnamon | | confectioners' sugar |
| | apricot glaze | | vanilla ice cream |
| | chocolate or caramel sauce | | fresh mint |
| | puff pastry, about 5 x 15 inches | | |

Wash, core, peel and halve the apples. Slice very thin and hold in lemon-water. If using frozen puff pastry, defrost on ungreased baking sheet. Dock pastry well. Melt brown sugar with water and brush on pastry. Sprinkle liberally with granulated sugar. Drain apples and place three across on pastry, overlapping in descending rows until pastry sheet is covered. Sprinkle lightly with cinnamon. Sprinkle baking sheet with water and bake at 425°F for 10 minutes. When cool, sprinkle with confectioners' sugar. Glaze briefly under broiler and brush with an apricot glaze. Cut in four equal portions and serve with vanilla ice cream and chocolate or caramel sauce. Garnish with fresh mint.

Old Mission Tavern

# Cherry Cobbler

| | | | |
|---|---|---|---|
| ½ C | butter | 1 C | sugar |
| 2 | eggs, beaten | ½ t | salt |
| 4 t | baking powder | 2 C | flour |
| 1 C | milk | 1 qt | pitted, sugared cherries |

In a bowl, cream the butter, add sugar and then the beaten egg. In another bowl, mix salt and baking powder well with flour. Alternately add flour mix and milk to egg-butter mixture. Put mixture in 9x13-inch pan and top with sugared cherries. Bake at 350°F for 45 minutes. Cherries will sink to bottom and crust will form on top.

Reflections

# Black Forest Cheesecake
With Cherry Sauce

## CRUST

| | | | |
|---|---|---|---|
| 2$^1/_2$ C | Oreo cookie crumbs | 2$^1/_2$ oz | melted butter |

Mix butter and crumbs. Spray cheesecake pan. Press in mixture.

## CHEESECAKE

| | | | |
|---|---|---|---|
| 2 lb | cream cheese | 1 lb | powdered sugar |
| $^2/_3$ C | flour | 8 | eggs |
| 6 oz | chopped dark chocolate | 1 t | vanilla |

Bring cheese to room temperature. Mix in processor or blender 5 minutes at low speed. Add sugar and mix 5 minutes more. Scrape down sides of bowl. Add flour and mix 5 more minutes. Scrape down sides of bowl. Add eggs one at a time while continuing to mix at low speed, pausing after 4 eggs to scrape sides of bowl again. Add vanilla and fold in chocolate. Pour mixture in prepared crust. Bake in a water bath for two and a half hours at 275°F. Turn off oven and let cake sit one hour before removing from pan. Let cool to room temperature, then refrigerate overnight.

## CHERRY SAUCE

| | | | |
|---|---|---|---|
| 3 C | canned dark sweet cherries | $^1/_4$ C | cherry brandy |
| 2 T | cornstarch | 2 T | water |

Prepare a paste of cornstarch and water. Bring cherries and brandy to a boil, add starch paste and stir until sauce thickens.

Tapawingo

# Apple Streusel Tart

(Makes one 11-inch tart)

Pastry

| | | | |
|---|---|---|---|
| 4 oz | butter | 2$^1$/$_3$ C | flour |
| $^1$/$_8$ t | salt | $^1$/$_3$ C | granulated sugar |
| 2 | eggs | | |

Chill butter in $^1$/$_4$-inch cubes. Put in food processor with dry ingredients, pulsing machine to produce coarse cornmeal consistency. Add eggs and process briefly. Knead on work surface to form two disks 1$^1$/$_2$ inches thick. Cover with plastic film and chill at least 1 hour. (Each disk makes one 11-inch tart).

BOTTOM LAYER FILLING

| | | | |
|---|---|---|---|
| 1$^3$/$_4$ lb | Granny Smith apples | 1 t | finely chopped lemon peel |
| 2$^1$/$_2$ T | granulated sugar | 1 T | butter |
| 2 T | Calvados or rum | $^1$/$_2$ t | vanilla extract |
| $^1$/$_8$ t | ground cinnamon | $^1$/$_8$ t | nutmeg |
| $^1$/$_4$ C | apricot preserves | | |

Peel, core and slice apples and place with lemon peel in covered pan and cook over low heat until consistency of thick apple sauce. Uncover and add remaining ingredients. Cook, stirring occasionally, until liquid has evaporated and mixture is very thick. Cool.

TOP LAYER FILLING

| | | | |
|---|---|---|---|
| 6 | apples | 1 T | cinnamon |
| $^1$/$_2$ C | chopped pecans | $^1$/$_4$ C | granulated sugar |
| $^1$/$_2$ C | dried tart cherries | 1 oz | bourbon |
| 2 oz | butter | | |

Peel, core and slice apples 1/4-inch thick. Combine with all but butter. Melt butter in pan and sauté apples until slightly soft. Cool.

## STREUSEL TOPPING

| | | | |
|---|---|---|---|
| ³/₄ C | all-purpose flour | 3 oz | unsalted butter |
| ³/₄ C | granulated sugar | ³/₄ C | finely chopped pecans |

Combine flour and sugar on work surface. Cut butter into small pieces and continue cutting until mixture resembles coarse meal. Work in the pecans and set aside.

## BAKING AND ASSEMBLY

Roll dough to fit 11-inch tart pan. Chill 2 hours. Preheat oven to 350°F. Pierce bottom with fork and line with parchment paper. Fill with beans to hold down pastry. Bake until pastry is "dry." Cool. Remove beans. Preheat oven to 375°F. Spread bottom-layer filling evenly in tart shell. Mound top-layer filling over it, then sprinkle with streusel topping. Bake about 30 minutes or until golden and bubbling. Serve warm with vanilla ice cream or cinnamon *crème Anglaise*.

Rose Room, Perry Hotel.

# Dutch Apple Pie

*(Makes 1 pie)*

| | | | |
|---|---|---|---|
| 1 | pie shell, pre-baked | 2¹/₄ lb | apples |
| ³/₄ C | sugar | ¹/₄ C | cornstarch |
| 1 T | cinnamon | 1¹/₃ C | flour |
| 5 oz | butter | 7 oz | brown sugar |

Peel, core and slice apples. Combine sugar, cornstarch and cinnamon and mix with apples. Layer into pre-cooked pie shell. Sift flour, cut in butter, add brown sugar and sprinkle over pie.

The Rowe

# Raspberry Cream Tart

### CRUST

| | | | | |
|---|---|---|---|---|
| 2 C | lightly toasted pecans | $^1/_3$ C | brown sugar |
| $^1/_4$ t | cinnamon | $^1/_8$ t | ground cloves |
| $^1/_4$ C | melted, unsalted butter | | |

Mix pecans, brown sugar, cinnamon, and cloves to coarse crumbs in food processor. Quickly add butter and mix. Pour crumb mixture into 9-inch spring-form pan, pressing crumbs evenly into bottom and sides. Chill 30 minutes. Bake at 350°F until brown (about 20 minutes). Cool completely.

### FILLING

| | | | | |
|---|---|---|---|---|
| 16 oz | softened cream cheese | $^1/_2$ C | heavy cream |
| $^1/_2$ C | sugar | 1 t | vanilla |

Beat cream cheese, cream, sugar and vanilla together until smooth. Pour filling into crust, cover with plastic wrap and refrigerate until firm—at least 4 hours and preferably overnight.

### TOPPING

| | | | | |
|---|---|---|---|---|
| 4 C | fresh raspberries | 1 T | cornstarch |
| $^1/_2$ C | sugar | 2 T | kirsch liqueur |

Take the largest and best berries and arrange on top of the chilled tart filling. Dissolve cornstarch in 2 oz of water. Crush remaining berries and combine in a saucepan with sugar and dissolved cornstarch. Stir over medium heat until mixture thickens and comes to a boil. Remove from heat and strain through a fine sieve to remove seeds. Stir in Kirsch and chill. Drizzle sauce over tart slices before serving.

Terry's Place

# Key Lime Pie

*(Serves 8)*

| | | | |
|---|---|---|---|
| 6 | egg yolks | $^1/_2$ C | lime juice |
| 1 | lime (zest only) | 8 | 3" graham-cracker shells |
| 14oz | sweetened condensed milk | | |

Combine ingredients until well blended and pour into graham-cracker shells. Bake 10 minutes at 350°F. Let cool. Chill and serve.

Windows

# Chocolate Paté

*(Serves 6-8)*

| | | | |
|---|---|---|---|
| 1 lb | semi-sweet chocolate | 1 C | coffee |
| 1 C | sugar | 12 oz | butter |
| 8 | eggs | | |

Boil coffee and sugar together until sugar has completely dissolved. Melt chocolate in double boiler and slowly add coffee. Mix well. Beat in butter a little at a time, alternating with eggs until everything is smooth and well blended. Pour into a greased loaf pan, bake in a water bath at 300°F for 2 to $2^1/_2$ hours. Serve warm with freshly whipped cream.

Top of the Park

# Grand Marnier Sabayon
## Over Fruit with Lemon Tuiles

*(Serves 4-6)*

### TUILES

| | | | | |
|---|---|---|---|---|
| 1¹/₂ C | granulated sugar | | 3 | large eggs |
| 1 C | unsalted butter | | 1¹/₂ C | all-purpose flour |
| | the zest of two lemons | | | |

Lightly cream butter and sugar. Add eggs one at a time, beating in each egg before adding the next. Add flour and zest, and beat until smooth. Pipe batter through a pastry bag onto a greased cookie sheet into desired shape. Bake at 350°F until light golden brown. (Tuile *means "tile" and each should be cookie-sized, thin and crisp. Classic French* tuiles *are often given a graceful curve by forming over a rolling pin while fresh from the oven before they crisp.*)

### SABAYON (Zabaglione)

| | | | | |
|---|---|---|---|---|
| 4 | egg yolks | | ¹/₄ C | granulated sugar |
| 1 oz | Grand Marnier | | | zest of ¹/₂ orange |
| 6 oz | heavy cream | | 1 | tuile per serving |
| | seasonal berries or fruit | | | |

Heat yolks and sugar in double boiler until very warm. Whip until yolks are pale yellow. Stir in Grand Marnier and zest. Whip cream and fold into above. Fill a wine or champagne glass with seasonal fruit or berries. Pour sabayon over fruit, garnish with lemon *tuiles*.

# Walloon Lake Inn

# La Tarte Tatin

*(Serves 8)*

PASTRY

| | | | |
|---|---|---|---|
| 1½ C | flour | 1 T | sugar |
| 1 | pinch salt | 4oz | cold unsalted butter |
| 2 T | shortening | ⅓ C | water |

Combine dry ingredients, work in butter and shortening and water as needed. Form inch-thick cake and chill at least an hour wrapped in plastic. Remove to room temperature several minutes before rolling to 1/8 inch. (Roll between sheets of plastic wrap or waxed paper to prevent sticking.)

FILLING

| | | | |
|---|---|---|---|
| 6 | lg. apples | 2 T | lemon juice |
| ¾ C | sugar, plus 1 T | 3 T | water |
| ½ t | nutmeg | ½ t | cinnamon |
| 1 t | lemon zest | 2 T | butter |

Peel, core and slice apples. Mix sugar, water, and 1 T lemon juice in an iron skillet (8-10 inch) and caramelize over high heat. (Use care that mixture does not burn, as caramelization occurs rapidly at proper temperature). Arrange apples on caramelized mixture in pan and sprinkle evenly with nutmeg, cinnamon, lemon zest, butter, and remaining lemon juice. Bake at 400°F for 30 minutes. Remove from oven, cover with pastry, slash top and bake at 425°F for 20 minutes more. Cool briefly and invert onto serving plate to remove from pan. If you cool too long and tarte sticks in pan; re-heat it gently on the stove to melt caramel. Glaze and cover with sauce (below).

GLAZE

| | | | |
|---|---|---|---|
| ⅓ C | apricot preserves | 1 T | Cognac |
| 1 T | water | | |

Combine and mix together thoroughly.

SAUCE

| | | | |
|---|---|---|---|
| 1 C | sour cream | 4 T | confectioners' sugar |
| ½ t | vanilla extract | | |

Combine and mix together thoroughly.

Weathervane

# Cheesecake

*(Makes one 10-inch cheesecake)*

CRUST

| | | | | |
|---|---|---|---|---|
| 2 oz | butter | | 1¹/₄ C | graham cracker crumbs |
| ¹/₄ C | sugar | | | |

Combine graham crackers and sugar. Cut in butter.

BATTER

| | | | | |
|---|---|---|---|---|
| 3¹/₂ oz | butter | | ¹/₂ lb | sugar |
| 1¹/₄ lb | cream cheese | | 4 | eggs |
| ¹/₂ C | sour cream | | 1 oz | cornstarch |
| ¹/₂ t | powdered vanilla | | ²/₃ C | milk |

Cream butter and sugar. Add cream cheese and eggs, then sour cream, cornstarch, vanilla and milk. Mix approximately two minutes. Mold crust into pie pan, pour in filling, and chill until set.

Windows

# Chocolate Mousse Olivia

| | | | | |
|---|---|---|---|---|
| 6 oz | bittersweet chocolate | | 6 oz | butter |
| 6 | eggs | | 1 C | finely chopped white chocolate |

Separate eggs. Melt bittersweet chocolate and butter over double boliler on low heat. Whip eggs whites until they form a soft meringue. Remove chocolate mixture from heat and beat in egg yolks. Gently fold together the egg whites and the chocolate-and-yolk mixture. Let stand 1 hour in refrigerator. Slowly melt white chocolate in top of double boiler and pipe out lattice work as demonstrated at Windows.

# Side Dishes, Bread, Etc.

## American Spoon Foods

## Holiday Stuffing

*(Fills an 18-lb. turkey)*

| | | | | |
|---|---|---|---|---|
| 6 oz | dried tart cherries | | 1 C | Madeira |
| 8 C | white-bread toast crumbs | | 1 ½ C | toasted pecan pieces |
| 1 C | finely chopped onion | | 1 C | finely chopped celery |
| 12 C | finely chopped shallots | | 12 C | sweet butter |
| 3 | crisp apples, coarsely chopped | | ½ C | golden raisins |
| ½ C | finely chopped flat-leaf parsley | | 2 T | dried tarragon |
| 1 T | dried thyme | | 10-12 | dried sage leaves, crumbled |
| 1 t | salt | | 1 t | freshly ground black pepper |

Let the cherries soak several hours (or overnight) in the Madeira. In a large bowl, combine the crumbs with them pecans. Drain the cherries, reserving the Madeira, and add them to the bread mixture. Melt butter in a skillet and saute the onion, celery and shallots until softened, and add to the bread mixture. Add the apples, raisins, herbs and seasonings and reserved Madeira. Toss well.

La Bécasse

# Acorn Squash Timbales
## With Savory Herb Sauce

*(Makes 8 timbales)*

### TIMBALES

| | | | |
|---|---|---|---|
| 1 | medium acorn squash | 1 C | heavy cream |
| 3 | eggs | 1 t | dried thyme |
| dash | nutmeg | | salt and pepper |
| pinch | each, of dried tarragon and coriander | | |

Pierce squash. Bake at 350ºF for 1 hour or until tender. Remove seeds and scoop squash into food processor bowl. Add cream, eggs, thyme, nutmeg, tarragon, and coriander. Season with salt and pepper. Process until smooth. Turn into 8 buttered 4-ounce timbale molds. Cover with buttered foil. Bake in hot water bath 40 minutes at 300ºF or until timbales are set.

### SAVORY HERB SAUCE

| | | | |
|---|---|---|---|
| 2 T | butter | 2 | shallots, minced |
| 2 T | flour | 1 C | dry white wine |
| 2 C | heavy cream | 3 oz | chevre, crumbled |
| 1 t | fresh lemon juice | 1 t | fresh minced parsley |
| dash | dried thyme, sage, rosemary, basil, tarragon | | |
| | salt and pepper to taste | | |

Saute shallots in butter until soft. Stir in flour. Gradually stir in wine; continue cooking, stirring constantly until mixture comes to a boil. Reduce heat and simmer five minutes. Stir in remaining ingredients. To serve, cover 8 eight plates with sauce; turn timbales out on top of sauce. Garnish with additional fresh minced parsley.

On the Edge

# Corn Pudding

*(Serves 2-4)*

| | | | |
|---|---|---|---|
| 1 T | unsalted butter | 2 C | fresh corn kernels |
| 1/2 C | heavy cream | 2 | eggs |
| pinch | cinnamon | 1 T | pure maple syrup |
| 1 T | diced red pepper | 1 T | diced green pepper |
| 1 | diced jalapeno pepper | 1 T | chopped fresh cilantro |
| | salt and pepper to taste | | |

Preheat oven to 375°F. Spread butter on a small baking dish and set aside. Puree 1 cup of the corn in a food processor. In a mixing bowl, beat together the cream, eggs, cinnamon, peppers, cilantro and maple syrup. Add the corn puree and remaining whole kernels and mix well, seasoning to taste with salt and pepper. Pour into baking dish, cover with foil, and bake in middle of oven for 45-50 minutes. (Pudding is done when skewer inserted in center comes out clean.)

Stafford's Bay View Inn

# Tomato Pudding

*(Serves 6)*

| | | | |
|---|---|---|---|
| 1 | #10 can stewed tomatoes | 1/2 C | brown sugar |
| 4 C | dried 1-inch bread cubes | | basil, thyme, salt, pepper to taste |

Drain tomatoes and place in mixing bowl. Add brown sugar and bread cubes, season to taste and mix well. Place in casserole, dot with butter, and bake at 350°F for 30-45 minutes. (Fresh tomatoes can be used instead of canned, but must be peeled, stewed and drained).

One Water Street

# Herb Duchesse Potatoes

(Serves 4-8)

| | | | |
|---|---|---|---|
| 3 lb | white potato, peeled and cooked | 4 | eggs |
| 1/2 | stick butter, melted | 1 t | basil |
| 1 t | rosemary | 1 | green onion, minced |
| | salt, pepper to taste | | |

Whip all ingredients together and place in pastry bag. Pipe into large rosettes and bake at 375°F until golden.

Windows

# Dauphinoise Potatoes

(Serves 6-8)

| | | | |
|---|---|---|---|
| 4 | potatoes, peeled and sliced paper thin | | |
| 1 1/2 C | whole cream | 1 1/2 C | milk |
| 9 | eggs | 2 | cloves crushed garlic |
| 1 C | shredded Swiss cheese | 1/4 C | grated Parmesan cheese |
| 1 T | butter | | |

In advance, mix cream, milk, and eggs in bowl; season with salt, pepper, and nutmeg. Set aside. Coat the inside of a 9-inch, stainless-steel, cake pan with butter and rub garlic cloves on inside of pan. Put sliced potatoes in pan. Pour on cream mixture until it barely covers potatoes. Sprinkle on cheeses. Bake at 325°F for 45-60 minutes.

## The Bluebird

# New Orleans Brabant Potatoes

*(Serves 6)*

| | | | |
|---|---|---|---|
| 3 lb | cooked, chilled redskins | 4 C | vegetable oil |
| 10 | scallions, sliced thin | 1 T | minced fresh garlic |
| 2 T | butter | 2 t | Lawrey's seasoned salt |
| 1 t | fresh ground black pepper | pinch | thyme |

Cut cooked potatoes into 3/4-inch cubes. Heat oil in tall saucepan and fry potatoes in batches until medium brown. Reserve potatoes. Heat butter to sizzling in a clean saucepan. Add garlic and cook until lightly browned. Add fried potatoes and scallions, toss for a minute. Add seasoned salt, pepper and thyme, and serve on a platter. (*These are regulars on the Sunday brunch menu at The Bluebird, where patrons call them "those garlic potatoes." A brabant is a plow in Belgium, and these will certainly satisfy the ploughman.*)

## The Authors

# Mom's Egg Noodles

*(Serves 8)*

| | | | |
|---|---|---|---|
| 4 | eggs | 3 T | half-and-half |
| 1 t | salt | 2 C | flour |

Beat eggs until light. Mix in half-and-half and salt. Stir in flour and finish by hand until the flour is thoroughly worked in. Divide dough into three equal parts on a floured board and roll each as thin as possible. Lay on floured counter and let dry some, then roll up as you would a jelly roll. Cut off half-inch slices and unroll strips onto counter to finish drying. Store in tins or, wrapped, in freezer. (*The Mom in question is Sherri's, who cooks these old-fashioned egg noodles by the gallon for family gatherings. She cooks her noodles in chicken broth, for a long time over low heat so they absorb the flavor and get buttery soft. At Mom's, all the Schabergs and Lovelaces heap them on the mashed potatoes, and one of Mom's grandsons microwaves any leftovers for breakfast.*)

# Smoked Turkey & Wild Rice Muffins

*(Makes 1 dozen)*

| | | | | |
|---|---|---|---|---|
| 4 T | butter | | $^1/_2$ C | finely chopped onion |
| $^1/_2$ t | minced fresh garlic | | 2 C | all-purpose flour |
| 1 T | baking powder | | 1$^1/_2$ t | salt |
| $^1/_2$ t | black pepper | | 1 C | milk |
| 2 | large eggs | | $^1/_4$ C | wild rice |
| $^3/_4$ C | chopped smoked turkey | | | |

Add rice to 1 cup of water in a heavy saucepan and simmer, covered, for 40 minutes or until grains burst and are tender. Let cool before using. Melt butter in a medium saucepan over moderate heat, add onion and garlic and cook 5-7 minutes, stirring occasionally, until soft. Remove from heat. Heat oven to 350°F. Line muffin tin with baking cups. Thoroughly mix baking powder, flour, salt and pepper in a large bowl. Whisk milk and eggs in another bowl. Stir in wild rice, turkey, and onion mixture. Pour over dry ingredients, folding in with a rubber spatula until all dry ingredients are moistened (batter will be stiff). Scoop batter into muffin cups, and bake 27-32 minutes, or until muffins are no longer moist in center. Let cool 5 or 10 minutes before turning out onto a rack. (*The Left bank serves many lunches consisting of these muffins, their Caesar Salad and a hot soup*).

Northern Delights

# No-Fat Cran-Orange Scones

*(Yields 6-12 scones)*

| | | | |
|---|---|---|---|
| 3¹/₂ C | soft whole-wheat flour | ¹/₂ C | oats |
| 1 t | salt | 1 t | baking powder |
| 1 t | baking soda | 1 t | caraway seeds, softened |
| ³/₄ C | dried cranberries | 1 C | plain, low-fat yogurt |
| ³/₄ C | milk | 2 T | honey |
| 1 | orange | 4 T | brown sugar |

Combine flour, oats, salt, baking powder, baking soda and caraway, and set aside. Soften cranberries by spritzing lightly with hot water, and set aside. Zest and chop orange, and combine with all remaining ingredients and the softened cranberries. Add the dry mixture to the yogurt mixture just until moistened. Do not overmix. Using a 2- or 3-ounce scoop, place mixture on greased, floured cookie sheet. Bake at 350°F. until lightly browned—about 10 or 15 minutes. *(This is one of many no-fat and low-fat items for which Jim Barnes's Northern Delights in Benzonia is known. All his bagels, scones, muffins and breads are made from organic, whole-wheat flours.)*

Rose Room, Stafford's Perry Hotel

# Zucchini Bread

*(Makes 2 loaves)*

| | | | |
|---|---|---|---|
| 1 C | salad oil | 2 C | sugar |
| 1 oz | vanilla extract | 3 | eggs |
| 1 t | salt | 1 t | baking soda |
| 1 t | baking powder | 3³/₄ C | flour |
| 1 t | cinnamon | 1¹/₄ C | grated zucchini |
| ¹/₂ C | grated carrots | 1 | 14-oz. can crushed pineapple |
| 1 C | walnuts, chopped | | |

Cream sugar and oil together. Add eggs and vanilla. Sift dry ingredients and add to sugar-oil mixture. Add zucchini, carrots and pineapple. Mix in chopped nuts. Grease two loaf pans and divide batter between them. Bake at 350ºF for about 1 hour or until test toothpick comes out clean.

Hose House Deli

# Award-Winning Greek Pizza

*(Makes 1 pizza)*

## DOUGH

| | | | | |
|---|---|---|---|---|
| 1 t | salt | | 1 t | sugar |
| 3 t | oil | | 2 t | dry yeast |
| 2 C | warm water | | 6 C | flour |

Combine salt, sugar, oil and water in a large mixing bowl. Add half the flour, add yeast, and mix thoroughly. Add remaining flour gradually until dough is not sticky to touch. Cover and set aside in a warm place until dough doubles in volume. Roll to form a 16 inch circle.

## TOPPINGS

| | | | | |
|---|---|---|---|---|
| 8 oz | pizza sauce | | 1 | lg. eggplant in $1/4$-inch slices |
| 8 oz | fresh spinach | | 1 | sm. onion, chopped |
| $1/2$ C | sliced black olives | | 4 oz | feta cheese, crumbled |
| 8 oz | mozzarella cheese | | | |

Assembly:

Preheat oven to 450ºF. Roll dough out to form 16-inch circle. Spread on sauce. Arrange eggplant slices atop sauce. Evenly distribute spinach, onions, olives and feta on top of eggplant. Top with mozzarella. Place pizza in preheated oven until crust is golden, about 20-30 minutes. *(This pizza was named "best exotic pizza" at the 1995 pizza convention in Las Vegas by* Pizza Today *magazine .)*

## Rose Room, Stafford's Perry Hotel

# Sun-dried Tomato Spread

*(Makes 1 quart)*

| | | | |
|---|---|---|---|
| 1 1/2 lb | cream cheese | 1/2 C | sun-dried tomatoes |
| 2 | green onions | | olive oil |
| | basil, thyme, oregano, marjoram, bay leaf | | |

Re-hydrate tomatoes in hot water, then soak overnight in a marinade of oil and herbs. Chop tomatoes and green onions in processor, combine with cream cheese in mixer with a paddle. (You can reserve the marinade for making your next batch of spread.)

## Roast and Toast

# Chicken Club Sandwich
With Pesto Mayonnaise and Prosciutto

| | | | |
|---|---|---|---|
| 2 C | mayonnaise | 1/4 C | pesto |
| 3/4 C | crumbled bleu cheese | 2 | thick slices fresh bread |
| 4 oz | grilled chicken breast | 1 | thin slice prosciutto |
| | thinly sliced onion and tomato | | leaf lettuce |

Mix mayonnaise, pesto and cheese thoroughly. (Makes enough for several sandwiches). Slice chick thinly. Spread mayo mix on bread, then layer on the tomato, prosciutto, onion, lettuce, and chicken. Season lightly with salt and pepper.

Cappuccino's

# Veggie Sandwich

*(Amounts are per sandwich)*

| | | | |
|---|---|---|---|
| 1 C | Portobello mushrooms | ¹/₂ C | Oriental vegetable mix |
| ¹/₈ C | chopped green pepper | 2 | slices toast |
| ¹/₄ C | chopped onion | 1 T | butter |
| 2 slices | Swiss cheese | | slaw dressing |

Saute mushroom, onion and vegetable mix in butter. Grill buttered toast slices topped with slices of cheese until cheese melts. Drizzle melted cheese with slaw dressing (*Cappuccino's uses Marzetti brand*) and sandwich the veggie mix between slices.

Cappuccino's

# Viking Breakfast Eggs

*(Yields one serving)*

| | | | |
|---|---|---|---|
| 3 | eggs | 2 t | butter |
| ¹/₄ C | smoked turkey | ¹/₄ C | smoked ham |
| 2 slices | Swiss, diced | | |

Saute meat in butter. Add cheese and let it start to melt. Add eggs. Scramble and cook. (*This makes a single serving at the restaurant, but John Dozier's servings are humongous, and you may find it sufficient for two ordinary mortals*).

# How to Cope with Being in Charge

If you've been appointed provisioner for a major event like a company conference or a family reunion or wedding, you might want professional help. Plenty of skilled and imaginative folks are standing by Up North: Traverse City's Pat Martel is a whiz with weddings and such, and caterers like Mary Boudjalis (Mary's Kitchen Port), Jackie Honea (Left Bank Cafe), and the Harbor Springs Gourmet can do wonders for your menu.

For total hands-off luxury, however, we'd summon an outfit called The Executive Selection in Traverse City. Talk about versatile! Led by owner Cathy Keelan, these intrepid folks can arrange everything from taxis and limos to table decorations and gift baskets. They can dress up your banquet, turn down your beds, and leave little custom-touch delicacies on every pillow. They'll put you in touch with caterers, inflate your balloons, and even organize your fun and games. We'll never forget the time they had dozens of highly-paid Fortune 500 executives at a Grand Traverse Resort conference having a ball out in the snow, seeing who could throw a frozen lake trout the farthest. After that they took them inside for some human bowling (don't even ask) and fun on the Velcro Wall. They'll even print maps and signs so your relatives and guests can find their way through the woods to your party. *The Executive Selection, 4171 Foxcraft, Traverse City. 616/938-3336.*

## The Morel: King of Spring

The morel mushroom is second only to the whitefish as the favorite food Up North. The morel is celebrated throughout Northern Michigan, and nowhere more extravagantly than each May in Boyne City, home of the annual Morel Mushroom Festival and its National Morel Hunting Championship. Top morellers sell their mushrooms to restaurants for as much as $15 a pound in a good year. They guard their secrets jealously, and charge good money to guide the inexperienced. Once you've learned enough to be bringing in several pounds of morels each spring, how do you make them last? We learned this simple method from Tapawingo's Pete Peterson: Wash then thoroughly dry them. Heat a generous amount of butter and quickly saute the morels over high heat, stirring until they're coated with butter but not shriveled. Remove to a foil-covered baking sheet to cool, then put the sheet in the freezer until morels are solid. Packed in sealed plastic bags, they keep in the freezer for months.

# Index

The Connoisseur Up North    **219**

# About the Authors

Graydon DeCamp earned a wide reputation for his entertaining, authoritative restaurant reviews in seven years of columns and features as senior editor and contributing editor of *Traverse, Northern Michigan's Magazine*. Restaurants and food represent a change of pace after his 21-year career in journalism in Cincinnati as a reporter, political columnist, city editor and magazine editor. He is no stranger Up North, however. He lived year-round in Traverse City while growing up, and has spent a lifetime of summers in both Michigan and Ontario. He has written books about the U. S. Naval Academy (*The Blue and Gold*, Arco, NY, 1974) and his former newspaper (*Old Lady of Vine Street, a Sesquicentennial History of The Cincinnati Enquirer*, 1991). This is his first book about food.

Sherri DeCamp, provides inside perspective on the hospitality industry from her work in corporate and association group sales in the Chicago market for Grand Traverse Resort. For five years in the 1980s she designed programs for a Cincinnati-based corporate leadership-training center, including menus, meals and other food events. She, too, knows Northern Michigan well, having sailed the coast from Holland to Mackinac each summer during a 14-year career in education downstate following college at Western Michigan University and a masters degree at MSU.

The DeCamps, who returned to Northern Michigan permanently in 1989, live in Elk Rapids. They are active in the region's arts community, as trustees of the Traverse Symphony (of which Graydon was president in 1994-5). Sherri has also served on the board of Company Dance Traverse and is active with the Make-A-Wish Foundation. Both are accomplished in the kitchen, and they value the region's boundless recreational opportunities partly for adventure's sake but also, as they say, "because it takes a very active life to let us eat as well as we want to."